T0116089

ƒP

Run the Other Way

Fixing the Two-Party System, One Campaign at a Time

Bill Hillsman

Free Press

New York   London   Toronto   Sydney

*f*P

FREE PRESS
A Division of Simon & Schuster Inc.
1230 Avenue of the Americas
New York, NY 10020

Copyright © 2004 by William G. Hillsman

All rights reserved, including the right of reproduction
in whole or in part in any form.

FREE PRESS and colophon are trademarks of Simon & Schuster, Inc.

For information about special discounts for bulk purchases,
please contact Simon & Schuster Special Sales:
1-800-456-6798 or business@simonandschuster.com

Designed by Christine Weathersbee

Manufactured in the United States of America

1   3   5   7   9   10   8   6   4   2

Library of Congress Cataloging-in-Publication Data

Hillsman, Bill.
    Run the other way : fixing the two-party system, one campaign at
a time / Bill Hillsman.
        p.   cm.
    Includes index.
    1. Politics, Practical—United States.   2. Political campaigns—
United States.   3. Political parties—United States.   4. United
States—Politics and government—1989–   .   I. Title.
JK1726.H55   2004
324.7'0973—dc22   2003064382

ISBN   978-1-4165-6833-9

In memory of my grandmother, Beatrice E. Cameron,
who taught me what was right, what was wrong,
and how to tell the difference.

Freedom is participation in power.
—*Cicero*

When the going gets weird, the weird turn pro.
—*Hunter S. Thompson*

☆ ☆ ☆ ☆ CONTENTS ☆ ☆ ☆ ☆

Contents

x

☆ ☆ ACKNOWLEDGMENTS ☆ ☆

Writing a book while running a small business is darn near impossible. For making it possible, I'd like to thank all the current and past employees of my company, North Woods Advertising, especially Jill Harrison, Greta Bergstrom, Rena Dundovic, Jim Cousins, Tracy McCoy, and Dawn Erlandson.

For their invaluable help on the manuscript and their vital encouragement during the writing process, I'd like to thank the incomparable Scott Burns, Matt Bai, Dara Moskowitz, Arianna Huffington, Neal Karlen, Katherine Lanpher, and Roy Sekoff—all better writers than me. Thanks to John Peter Larson, who helped put the deal together. And a special thanks to Tom Spain, without whom this book would be not only unpublished but unpublishable.

Thanks to my best friends, attorneys Rocky Chrastil and Roy Ginsburg, who along with our pal Jon Steinberg try to keep me out of trouble, and occasionally succeed. Thanks also to my brothers Thom, Bob, Jim, John, Bucky, and Michael, who try to get me into trouble and—despite the efforts of my sister Patti—usually succeed.

Thanks also to all the supportive friends and companions who put up with me during political campaigns and/or authorship: Stacey Ranum, Barb Struck Rothmeier, Susan Sorensen, Kristine Larsen Spanier, Martha Ross Parker, Amy Buchanan, and especially Pilar Gerasimo, who believed in this project long before I did.

As every creative person knows, some of one's best thinking and writing gets done away from an office or a desk. I'd like to thank the places (and people therein) which kept me sane, well fed, and adequately lubricated through most of these campaigns and the writing of this book: all the folks at Eli's, Lowell Pickett at the Dakota, La Toscana, Le Cirque

Acknowledgments

Rouge, Nora's, Auriga, DuJour's, Il Panino, Nokomis Grill, the Sunset Marquis, and Chateau Marmont.

Many thanks to mentors of mine in the advertising field: Tom McElligott, Ron Anderson, Dick Thomas, Jim Lacey, David Bell, and Robb Besteman. And to the amazing writers, art directors, musicians, actors, producers, editors, and directors I've been privileged to work with: Luke Sullivan, Bob Barrie, Jarl Olsen, Tom Lichtenheld, Pete Smith, Tom Donovan, Jelly Helm, Lesley Chilcott, Laura Howard, Scott Burns, Peter Berg, Craig McNamara, Judy Wittenberg, Bill Whitney, Dan Mackaman, Renee Valois, Greg Cummins, Kirk Hokanson, Matt Quast, Paul Schupanitz, Pam Mariutto, Brooke Kenney, Gary LaMaster, Glen Wachoviak, Jeff Jones, Anne Swarts, Scott Ferril, Wendie Malick, John Williams, Bernadette Sullivan, Harlan Saperstein, Scott McCullough, Gary Rue, Leslie Ball, Johnny Hagen, Mike Ruekberg, Steve Kramer, and Bob Hest. (My apologies to the many others I'm sure I've inadvertently overlooked.) This work is as much theirs as mine.

Thanks to the brave candidates, clients, and staff members who recognized that, sometimes, the only safe thing is to take a chance: the late and sorely missed Paul, Sheila, and Marcia Wellstone, Jesse and Terry Ventura, Arianna Huffington, Ted Forstmann, Alan Page, Tony and Erica Bouza, John Hickenlooper and Helen Thorpe, Dean and Sue Barkley, Mike and Ann Ciresi, Roberta Walburn, Ralph Nader, Winona LaDuke, Theresa Amato and Todd Main, Doug and Denesse Johnson, Laura Boyd, Tracy Beckman, Jack Ryan, David Bradley Olsen, Chris Gates, Doug Friedline, John Woedele, David Ruth, Sean Pittman, Chris Coleman, Ole Tweet, Mark Blackwell, Chris Neugent, Brett Carver, Jeff Hoke, and especially Maureen Hooley Bausch, who also encouraged me to write this book.

Props to my coconspirators in trying to make the world a better place: Patrick Caddell, Marc Cooper, John Richard,

Acknowledgments

Mike Casper, Michael Moore, Joanne Doroshow, Aaron Sorkin, Kari Moe, Arick Wierson, Russell Mokhiber, Mike Erlandson, Steve Cobble, Paul Taylor, Micah Sifry, and the late Scott Shuger.

Thanks to all the friends I met at Harvard University's Institute of Politics: Senator David Pryor, Jennifer Phillips, Cathy McLaughlin, Eric Andersen, Julie Schroeder, Ben Dobbs, Christian Flynn, Gordon Li, Juleanna Glover Weiss, Callie Crossley, Chuck and Linda Robb, Ron Mazzoli, Jake Lentz, Adam Wienner, Betsy Sykes, Justin Gest, Previn Warren, Ganesh Sitaraman, Alex Jones, and especially Seth Gitell and David Nyhan (a Red Sox game and enough beers with Nyhan and you'll know where all the bodies are buried in Boston).

And of course, thanks to my editor at Free Press, Dominick Anfuso, and his more-than-able assistants throughout this long process, Kristen McGuinness and Wylie O'Sullivan. Last but not least, thanks to everyone at The Lazear Agency, particularly Christi Cardenas and my indefatigable agent, Jonathon Lazear.

☆ ☆ ☆ INTRODUCTION ☆ ☆ ☆

These are notes from the underground of American politics.

As much as I love Aaron Sorkin's televised portrayal of politics, *The West Wing,* it presents an unrealistic, idealized picture of our government. The reality is much closer to *The Sopranos*—escapades in raw ambition, with professional political hit men operating in the shadows and out of the public's view to maintain a vise-like grip on political power and to eliminate any threats to the two political parties' profitable business territories.

When you work for rebel, underdog candidates, like I do, even the occasional victory is one success too many as far as the established political firmament is concerned. By telling the truth about the current state of our politics, I've managed to antagonize both major political parties and make enemies of practically all the practitioners of politics in Washington, D.C.

For nearly fifteen years now, what I call Election Industry, Inc. has tried to put me out of commission. Beyond the whisper campaigns, the character assassinations, and the political backstabbings, I've put up with hate mail, broken windows, and menaces to my personal safety. As many of the candidates I've worked with realize, when you threaten the system, you get threatened.

Maybe a smarter person would just give up.

But you and I and those few brave candidates willing to challenge the existing system can't afford to give up. If we check out of the system (to slightly alter the phrase heard often from America's commander in chief), the political terrorists win.

This book is not just a memoir from memory. It is also a handbook for the new, developing political landscape, full of ways and means by which we still *can* win.

Introduction

Within these pages, you'll discover:

- How political parties control candidates, and why it's hard for good people to run for office anymore
- How big money negatively influences our politics, and how to win without it
- What political advertising can learn from commercial advertising, and how campaigns can more effectively develop messages and communicate with citizens
- How political professionals use negative advertising to intentionally hold down voter turnout, and the best ways to respond
- Why the two major political parties persist in shutting out new candidates, new parties, new viewpoints, and new ideas—despite the fact that Americans are clearly looking for more choices and that America has a long-standing tradition of multiparty elections
- How to analyze and evaluate (the mostly worthless) political polls

If a Paul Wellstone or a Russ Feingold can still be elected to the United States Senate, then eliminating child poverty in America or providing comprehensive health care to all our citizens is not an impossible dream. If a former professional wrestler can prove that the American Dream is still alive by becoming governor of our 21st-most-populated state, then getting elected is not beyond any citizen's grasp.

We have to keep challenging our own political system in order to make it all that it can be. That is the essence of participative democracy. We can't do what the power brokers of Election Industry, Inc. want us to do—grow discouraged, give up, and drop out.

After more than 225 years as a nation, it's too late to stop now.

Election Industry, Inc.

Americans own the greatest political system in the world. It works wonderfully well for everyone involved, except two groups of people:

Voters. And candidates.

Political parties, pollsters, political consultants, fundraisers, media mavens, junk mailers, spammers, special interest groups, lobbyists, and various other meretricious sorts all profit handsomely from our current political system.

Who pays for it? You. And me. And, of course, any candidate brave enough to run for public office.

After over a dozen years trying to upgrade political communications, I have come to understand that some of the most fearsome obstacles our candidates face are their own political parties and Washington, D.C.–based political consultants.

Most political consultants and both major political parties

treat candidates with disdain. They see candidates as virtually interchangeable: wind-up bad actors who would all be president if they could only follow the party's or the consultant's simple (but brilliant!) instructions, stand in the right place and recite their lines without drooling, tripping, or peeing in their pants.

They represent our politics at its worst: from party operatives to pollsters to direct mail merchants to media consultants to general strategists, the overwhelming majority of political consultants are a craven and narrow-minded bunch who would be failures in nearly every other field. They are hired guns with no soul and an inability to shoot straight (both ethically and functionally). They are disloyal to a fault, as quick to turn on a candidate or a cause as they are to be hired by one.

They give hucksterism a bad name.

Collectively, I call this monolith "Election Industry, Inc." Like the infamous "military-industrial complex" (but not nearly as productive), it is an inside-the-Beltway collective of toadies, fakes, crooks, character assassins, racketeers, party apologists, false scientists, phony experts, self-aggrandizers, backscratchers and backstabbers (often embodied in the same person). Election Industry, Inc. drives up the cost of our elections and drives down the number of people who participate in them. The people who populate it concern themselves with only two things: their own self-preservation, and money.

Election Industry, Inc. has killed some of our best candidates and kept many, many more of our best and brightest people from ever considering a run for office or a stint in public service. It owns and runs the two-party oligarchy that controls our country and refuses to let anyone outside its dominion near the levers of power. It makes the rules and legislates against new people, new political parties, new ideas, and new points of view.

The idiot wind blowing out of Washington is so manifest and so out-of-touch with the rest of the country that it is no wonder Election Industry, Inc.'s political advice is of little use to anyone but incumbents already ingratiated to their system. And with the advantages for incumbents that Election Industry, Inc.—and the incumbents themselves—have built into the system, perhaps it should be called ReElection Industry, Inc. Given their money and news media advantages, a consultant would have to give egregiously bad advice to ever have an incumbent lose.

Election Industry, Inc. likes to see its incumbents re-elected, because they are already subordinated to the system. Elected officials who are used to being treated like royalty in Washington have little incentive to disturb the system that rewards them.

Political consultants and the other members of Election Industry, Inc. almost always align themselves exclusively with one party or the other. They brag about won/loss ratios, never stopping to consider that in elections with only two candidates that must have a victor, even a coin-flipper on a hot streak can do somewhat better than 50 percent. If you think the revolving door between Congress and lobbyists is confusing, try to track the back-and-forthing among the two major political parties and the denizens of Election Industry, Inc. Pollsters recommend political consultants and vice-versa. Political party operatives refer pollsters and political consultants to candidates, then turn around and go to work for the polling firms and consultants, or vice-versa.

Election Industry, Inc. is the chief reason why so little of value gets done in Washington to solve our most pressing problems, and why few people outside this one-industry town feel connected to our federal government. Social Security? Health care? Child hunger? Budget deficits? Fixing our schools? All of these are little more than political and rhetorical footballs for the players of the system.

Perhaps most frightening of all is that Election Industry, Inc. is intent on becoming one of our biggest exports. Like an old-time tonic salesman finished with the fleecing of one town and moving on to the next, Election Industry, Inc. has set its sights on other countries, hoping to control their elections the way they control ours in America and using the same bag of tricks: phony polls, expensive media campaigns, negative and dishonest advertising, and other tactics designed intentionally to hold down voter turnout.

Is it any wonder people outside our borders are less than enchanted with America?

In American politics, winning is everything. It is the ultimate zero-sum, winner-take-all game. As far as Election Industry, Inc. is concerned, to win is to survive, and winning automatically validates whatever tactics you used to get there.

Election Industry, Inc. is a vast and mendacious enterprise that has fooled all but the smartest and bravest candidates into believing that their way is the only way. Using the power of money and media, it is debasing our democracy and aligns itself against the best parts of our nature. Election Industry, Inc. is an enemy of the people, with colossal advantages and odds that are overwhelmingly in its favor.

This is how we beat it.

Wellstone 1990

In 1990, Election Industry, Inc.'s stranglehold on American democracy started to loosen.

Under a headline reading "Political Consultants May Be Election's Big Losers," the late Bob Squier, dean of the Democratic media consultants and a charter member of Election Industry, Inc., was criticized for doctoring a newspaper headline that appeared in one of his commercials for Ann Richards during the Texas gubernatorial campaign, helping to snatch defeat from the jaws of victory. The article chided him for not paying more attention, and noted that (like most Election Industry, Inc. practitioners) he was working on a dozen gubernatorial and U.S. Senate races in 1990. Of course, in keeping with the forthright and stand-up nature of Election Industry, Inc., Squier apologized only after he was caught, then went on to blame the whole mess on someone else in his firm.

Randall Rothenberg's *New York Times* lead read, "The big

losers in Tuesday's elections may have been Washington insiders—the major league political consultants whose awkward advertisements and antics damaged their reputations and, in some cases, their candidates." Rothenberg pointed out that besides doctoring source material for their ads, major Washington consultants were caught using identical ads in different states for different candidates. Smith & Haroff, a big-time Republican consulting firm, was caught making up an entire phony *"Birmingham News"* newspaper article in the Alabama gubernatorial race. The article quoted another Republican member of Election Industry, Inc. bemoaning the fact that the Washington consultants could no longer "pull the wool over the voters' eyes."

The *New York Times* began its editorial entitled "Dirty Political Ads, Reconsidered" with this: *"Filthy campaigning can be fatal to politicians who practice it.* This notion has been more a prayer than an axiom. Then came Minnesota." Describing the ads that helped unseat U.S. Senator Rudy Boschwitz as "clean, and funny, extraordinary political comedy," the piece concluded that Boschwitz's "loss offers a welcome cautionary tale for those who campaign in the sewer."

Those were our ads, ads which my firm, North Woods Advertising, created for Paul Wellstone, the surprise winner in the Minnesota Senate race. It was my first major political campaign, and Paul's second run for statewide office. We were outspent by the incumbent Senator Boschwitz's campaign by a margin of over four to one. And in the days following the election, we had only begun to realize how profoundly we had rattled the cages of Election Industry, Inc.

Paul Wellstone walked into my office in the fall of 1989. I was vice president and creative director of a small Minneapolis ad agency.

"I'm thinking about running for the United States Senate next year," he told me.

I replied the way most Minnesotans would at the time: unconvincingly. "That's great, Paul."

He continued. "I understand you need advertising to run for the Senate."

In what would prove to be the first of many tutorials on the value of mass media, I explained to Paul that this was probably a good idea, since the huge majority of Minnesotans had never heard of him, despite his loss in a race for state auditor in 1982. It was a race in which Wellstone, a first-time candidate, talked more about foreign policy than state fiscal issues.

After I finished, a long silence ensued. Wellstone was a fervent believer in grassroots politics and local organizing. He didn't like and didn't trust advertising.

Paul began hemming and hawing a bit. He looked at the floor. He looked at his shoes. Finally, he looked at me.

"You're the only person I know in advertising."

And with that rousing endorsement, I was handed my first opportunity to do battle against Election Industry, Inc.

I knew Wellstone from my days at Carleton College, a small liberal arts school in rural Minnesota, forty miles south of the Minneapolis/St. Paul metropolitan area, where he was a professor of political science. I never took any political science courses in college, so I never had Wellstone for a teacher. That was OK with me. Paul didn't believe in grades and therefore gave everybody in his classes A's. Despite the fact that my grade-point average certainly could have used the boost, I really wasn't interested in politics or government.

It was probably OK with Paul, too. He was one of a cadre of activist professors on campus who would, according to the fashion of the time, periodically call for a strike to bring attention to some kind of injustice. I can't remember if it was due to the bombing of Hanoi or the mining of the port of Haiphong during the Vietnam War, but Wellstone and some other professors called for a moratorium on classes in the spring of 1972, during my freshman year.

Wellstone spotted me late one beautiful spring morning as I walked across campus, a case of empty Old Milwaukee beer bottles on my shoulder. I was on my way to refill the case at the municipal liquor store in town.

"Hillsman!" Paul yelled. (It's a small campus, and while I had never taken a class of Paul's, my two best friends were Wellstone acolytes. So I knew Paul socially.)

"You're coming to the teach-in this afternoon, aren't you?"

Now there is something you must understand about Minnesota. Winter pretty much coincides with the school year, insinuating itself in late September and generally lingering into May. Fall is frosty, and what passes for spring is generally windy, muddy, and wet with melting snow pack and rain. Good weather at any time of the year is rare. Yet for the past number of days, our little part of Minnesota had been blessed with some of the most beautiful warm and sunny spring days the campus could remember.

"No, Paul, I'm not," I hollered back. "I'm going to do exactly what my friends and I have been doing every day since you cancelled classes. We're going to get a bunch of beer and drink it and play coed softball all afternoon."

Then I made the solidarity fist that many East Coast Carleton students had learned from their older brothers and sisters, who had shut down Columbia University and other eastern colleges in recent years.

"But I want you to know that we're 100 percent behind what you're doing, and we all hope you can keep this up as long as possible!"

Wellstone 1990

Starting right then, Paul never could decide if I was a total cynic, a complete wiseass, or something else entirely.

In fact, by 1990, I was something of an idealist. An idealist with a theory.

As an ad exec, I had wondered for the past ten years why political advertising was so desperately bad, and I began to pay more attention to political ads to find out why. I had studied Ronald Reagan's 1984 reelection campaign, which was handled by a number of well-respected advertising practitioners, and George Bush's 1988 campaign, in which he utilized some very effective ads against the Democratic nominee, Massachusetts Governor Michael Dukakis. I had also noticed that Republicans generally had more money to spend on campaigns and seemed to understand communications better—and therefore spent their money better—than Democrats.

But most of the really good advertising and communications people I knew—the "creative people," in ad parlance—were not Republicans. They tended to lean more Democratic. Which got me wondering: what if you were able to do really good political ads, political ads that people actually watched and paid attention to and talked about? Didn't it stand to reason that ads people actually watched would be more effective than the usual political claptrap, which required a lot of money and repeated airings to somehow get people to even notice them?

Paul Wellstone's campaign would be my chance to find out.

I was confident Wellstone was the kind of candidate whose positions would appeal to many of my creative friends. I also knew from personal experience that he was a terrifically convincing and passionate speaker, especially in small group settings. And since Paul had no idea what role advertising played in a statewide campaign, it would be a perfect opportunity to test some of my theories about political advertising without a lot of resistance. (Or so I thought).

But what about money? Paul didn't have any. He had never tried to raise the kind of money a U.S. Senate candidate spends. The incumbent was a self-made millionaire who would "budget" whatever figure was necessary to keep his seat. $6 million, $8 million, even $10 million was not out of the question. How could we ever compete against a spending disadvantage like that?

The answer was to recruit the best possible people I could find. People who would not work on the campaign for less than their usual freelance rates were easy to eliminate. But others heard out my theory, and wanted the chance to show the world that creative political advertising was not an oxymoron. And many of us felt Paul Wellstone was the right kind of candidate for the time, and working for him was the right thing to do.

This would be one of the first times anyone had attempted to take the vagaries of politics and put them into a true marketing communications strategy and discipline. I began to construct an overall integrated communications strategy, wrote memos to the campaign, and began developing budgets and media plans. In short, my ad hoc team treated the Wellstone campaign the same way we would work on a commercial client.

Then the bad news started to roll in.

The campaign was in a shambles. Paul had been through three campaign managers and was on his fourth. There was no clear chain of command, committee upon committee had been formed to confuse every conceivable purpose, and fundraising was slow to the point of being nonexistent.

The conventional wisdom said that Boschwitz would be unbeatable, especially since his fellow Republican, U.S. Senator David Durenberger, had won handily in 1988. Only the most diehard, tunnel-visioned, and blinkered Democrats in the state actually believed Boschwitz could be defeated, and precious few of them were willing to back their opinion with a contribution, leaving us with no money to produce any of the dozens of good ideas we were creating for the campaign.

None of the big names in the Democratic Party wanted to challenge Boschwitz, but Paul still had to endure a Democratic primary against the state agricultural commissioner, Jim Nichols, who had no money (even less than us), no campaign organization, and no party endorsement. But heading into August, Paul still couldn't shake Nichols.

Unbeknownst to me, the campaign was getting all sorts of back channel, surreptitious advice from the usual knotheads of Election Industry, Inc. Paul didn't know who to listen to, and neither did his inexperienced campaign staff. In early August, we had shot footage for two commercials, and by the middle of the month, we had edited the first one, "Fast Paced Paul." Because it was so different from the usual run-of-the-mill political ads, the campaign was scared to death and refused to run it. Instead, the campaign had run a couple of the most cringingly bad political commercials ever made, including one spot on the issue of abortion starring Wellstone's teenage daughter, Marcia. Most bad political ads are simply ignored. This one was so wretched it was literally costing Paul support and making his numbers go backwards.

Wellstone himself was no fan of political advertising and wanted to put all the campaign's emphasis on grassroots campaigning and organizing. There was one problem: it wasn't working. With the primary rapidly approaching, Wellstone, the prohibitive favorite, was in danger of losing to an opponent who had done barely any campaigning whatsoever.

Now that his survival was in grave doubt, I tried one final

11

tutorial to try to get Wellstone to understand the necessity for our television strategy.

"Paul, you've just spent an entire month going all around the state. You've been campaigning sixteen, eighteen hours a day, usually seven days a week. You've met a lot of people and shaken a lot of hands. Now imagine it's the evening of August 31st. I can put one TV commercial on the air that night and reach more people in thirty seconds than you've reached traveling around the state in the past thirty days."

The argument failed to impress him. Rationalism failed to convince the college professor. He just plain didn't like advertising, and he really didn't like the kinds of ads we were pitching to the campaign—he thought they were silly and made a mockery of the process. When I pressed the argument further with the campaign staff, I was told Paul and the party elders didn't think the ad we had put together made him look "senatorial" enough.

"Senatorial!" I snorted. "The guy is built like a midget middle linebacker. He has hair like Harpo Marx and walks like Groucho. He refuses to wear suits and he's allergic to ties. And forget about long-sleeved shirts—if you can get him out of a muscle shirt and into even a short-sleeved dress shirt, it's like negotiating *détente*. It would take all the special effects George Lucas has in his bag of tricks to make Paul Wellstone look senatorial!"

What Paul and his staff couldn't see is something many of us professionals had discovered during the shooting and editing of the footage: the camera loved him. The camera embraces some people and stiffarms others. To the naked eye, Paul wasn't a very photogenic person, but for some intangible reason the camera fully captured his natural enthusiasm and good-heartedness—qualities that made him exactly the kind of person you would be comfortable with in your living room.

And in politics, the campaign exists on TV. In your living room.

Finally, out of desperation or by mistake, and with only a few days left before the primary, the campaign put "Fast Paced Paul" on the air. The voters immediately responded, and Paul won the primary election handily, with 60 percent of the vote to Agricultural Commissioner Jim Nichols's 35 percent.

The former college wrestler had legitimized himself as a contender.

My team was jazzed with the momentum generated by "Fast Paced Paul" and by his primary victory. Every time I came up with a new assignment there was suddenly somebody with open arms ready to accept it. Directors and production companies were donating their time and their services. Voice-over talents and actors were making themselves available. Everyone was getting paid something, but no one was getting paid much. (Me least of all. It took two years to collect the money owed us by the campaign.) People were excited about Paul's candidacy, especially those in the advertising and artistic communities, and wanted to be a part of the campaign. This was about love, not money. Whatever we needed, people figured out a way to get it done.

With our basic message established—we don't have money, Boschwitz does, so Boschwitz is going to try to buy the election—and with the contagious enthusiasm of "Fast Paced Paul" brimming out of TV sets across the state, we turned our attention to a follow-up ad, something we could produce fast and cheap. I had seen a demonstration of some of the new video "morphing" techniques at a local production house. The technique was simple, seamless and arresting. It was also fast. We decided to work up an idea using the technique with standard head shot photos of Boschwitz and Wellstone.

Paul had to come into a recording studio to read the voice-over without benefit of seeing the picture. By this point, he was more familiar with doing radio recordings, for which the scripts were self-contained and made sense on their own accord. Recording for the new TV spot threw Paul.

Paul felt that he had been burned once before when he followed our direction on "Fast Paced Paul"—we didn't exactly explain to him what we were doing, because I was sure he'd refuse—so he wanted to know precisely what he was getting into this time. Ever protective of his credibility, and worried about the veracity of the spot, Paul kept stumbling on the punch line. Even if it was joking, he was reluctant to do what the script called for: say he was better looking than Boschwitz. What Paul wasn't seeing is that it is so out of character for any political candidate to make this kind of self-aggrandizing claim that it was funny in context, and made fun of the whole political advertising game. It was especially ludicrous for the unsenatorial-looking Wellstone to make such a bald-faced claim. But even after we got it recorded, the "better-looking" line was the one line Paul and the campaign later told us they wanted removed. All the typical political minds and the conventional thinkers who had come out of the woodwork after we won the primary were now not shy about advising this first-time candidate—behind our backs—about exactly what he should do next.

The lessons of the unnecessary battle to get the first commercial on the air had clearly been forgotten, and they were second-guessing us already on commercial #2, which was just a placeholder anyway. I interceded and simply told Paul and the campaign that the commercial would air as it was written and produced, or not at all. (If it didn't air, I knew the campaign didn't have anything else to put on the air.) Fortunately, the Wellstone campaign was beginning to grasp the concept of momentum, as fundraising and positive feedback from volunteers and voters continued to grow. The commercial aired, but it was beginning to look like we were going to have to spend more time fighting our own campaign than Boschwitz's.

As we created more ads, more and more people began to warm to Wellstone, and the word of mouth and momentum were inching him closer and closer to Boschwitz, who had so far refused even to acknowledge this upstart challenger. Then, seemingly overnight, in mid-October, a *Minneapolis Star Tribune* poll showed Paul trailing Boschwitz by only 3 points—a statistical dead heat.

Those poll results awakened a slumbering giant. Boschwitz's campaign finally kicked into high gear. There would be no more ignoring the opponent by the Boschwitz camp. A U.S. Senate seat was in play here, and Boschwitz knew he would never hear the end of it from his cronies in the Senate if he lost to this unknown, hyperactive escapee from academia.

Despite his personal riches, Boschwitz had been admired for years in Washington for his prowess as a legendary fundraiser. And once he cranked up his money machine, the dollars rolled in. Boschwitz had been so successful at fundraising, the Republicans had him author an internal memo to other Republicans, telling them how to do it. It was an amazingly cynical document, explaining to other candidates how to give big contributors special stamps to mark their mail for preferential treatment, and how to wear colored shirts while walking parade routes, shirts that would show sweat stains and thus signify you were "working hard." Having recognized the value of advertising—especially direct mail—to his plywood business's success, Boschwitz was quick to apply these same techniques to his political fundraising. His "personal" fund-raising letters were always autopenned simply "Rudy," with a smiley face drawn next to the signature.

It might have been phony and it might have been simple-minded, but it was effective. While most incumbents would begin fundraising for their reelection about two years out from Election Day, Boschwitz would start fundraising for the next election just as soon as the last one ended. In the four years after his reelection in 1984, Boschwitz raised nearly $2 million—during a time when most campaigns would be dormant. When 1990 dawned, he had a $6.5 million war chest—enough money to scare off all of the potential high-profile Democratic challengers.

Now it was time to put that money to work and crush this antic upstart, this interloper. Earlier in the year, Boschwitz had run positive ads, touting how his work as a senator had bene-fited not just Minnesota, but all of America. But the time had come to put the nice-guy symbols away. It wasn't smiley-face time anymore. It was clobberin' time.

First the Boschwitz campaign peddled to reporters the fact that Paul had been arrested during political protests. Then they went on the attack over Wellstone's liberalism and desire to fund practically every government do-gooder program ever heard of.

Boschwitz's first attack ad scored a direct hit. It ripped into Wellstone for being a free-spending liberal who would squander Minnesotans' hard-earned tax money in Washington. A dollar bill appeared on screen, and gradually a frizzy-haired Wellstone replaced George Washington on the dollar bill.

I tried to spin our way out of this one. "Look," I told the reporters. "One of the tests for an ad's effectiveness is whether you can watch the ad without the sound track and still get the point and the story. If Boschwitz wants to run an ad equating Paul Wellstone with the father of our country, we may send him a few contributions ourselves to keep running it." But the attack was effective. Not only did it paint Wellstone as an unreconstructed, free-spending liberal, its most damaging image was the dated, frizzy-haired photo, which reinforced the notion of Wellstone as a hippie protester—anything but senatorial.

The next incoming missile was an ad showing a farmer tossing clumps of manure into a truck, and discussing how Wellstone wasn't being honest about not raising taxes while still funding all his pet programs. "In my job, we deal with that sort of thing all the time," he'd say dismissively, forking another load of dung into the truck.

Again, I tried to spin our way out of it, declaring that this must certainly be a Republican farmer, because not too many working farmers would be out there pitching horse crap in an expensive shearling coat and a white Stetson cowboy hat. But I knew most viewers wouldn't make those connections.

The ads became more and more negative and more and more frequent. Boschwitz started running a series of ads designed to "define" Wellstone as an enemy of children, someone who wanted to end Medicare, and a free spender who would double the national debt. We called them the "Who is this guy?" ads, because each one started out with a photo of Paul and a person's hand covering the photo as the announcer says, "Who is this guy?" One of the spots went like this:

Who is this guy who wants the federal bureaucracy to take over the American medical system? Who would take Medicare money from the seniors who need it so much and use it to fund his socialized health care plan? Who would eliminate Medicare coverage while doubling our personal income taxes? Who is he? Paul Wellstone. Not too smart for a college professor.

The ads were full of falsehoods, distortions of Paul's positions, and wild inaccuracies. One of the major daily newspaper reporters wrote, "This may be the most misleading political ad to appear in the state this year . . . nearly every major claim in this ad is inaccurate, misleading or distorted."

But the money machine didn't care. It kept chugging forward, and the attack strategy of Election Industry, Inc.—run the ads until the viewers are sick of them, and then run them some more—was taking its toll. As one viewer said to me late in the campaign, "I saw thirty minutes of Rudy Boschwitz commercials last night, interrupted by a little bit of *Cheers*."

By the Friday before the election, the newspaper polls now had us trailing Boschwitz by nine points. I didn't believe the spread was that large, and we also were confident we could get as many as five of those points back with the campaign's get-out-the-vote effort. Every successful campaign is a combination of the air war—media—and the ground war—volunteers. Our ads and media strategy had put Paul into a position to win, despite the onslaught of big-money political ads. Now Paul's long history as an organizer was about to become a big asset: we had hoards of volunteers ready to hit the streets over the final weekend, the Monday before the election, and Election Day itself.

If we didn't win, though, we were going to go down swinging. To give support to the get-out-the-vote effort, we ran a large newspaper ad the morning before Election Day, designed to motivate both our voters and our volunteers. The headline read: "If Your Answer Is Yes to Six or More of These Questions, Get Off Your Butt and Vote for Paul Wellstone." The ad listed Wellstone's core positions on a variety of issues, all of them posed as questions in a way that most Minnesotans would answer "yes" to.

Meanwhile, the volunteers were out in force. As I drove to my office during the morning rush hour, I was pleasantly surprised to see Wellstone supporters out in large numbers, doing "visibilities": holding up signs above freeway overpasses and on busy street corners. If retail politics and volunteerism still count for anything in this day and age of multimillion-dollar ad budgets, I thought to myself, we are at least going to give Boschwitz a run for his money.

Led by a young and indefatigable volunteer named Liz Borg, campaign workers toiled round the clock, many without any sleep and well into Election Day, doing literature drops and making phone calls and arranging to drive shut-in voters to the polls.

Then it was Election Day, and I did the only thing I'm any good for on Election Day. I voted. And waited.

The Minnesota Democratic Party's election night celebration was the first one I had ever attended, and I've since found out they're pretty much all alike: hotel ballrooms with cash bars, too many people, and not enough bartenders. I made a couple of trips up to the hotel room where Paul and his wife Sheila were sequestered with their kids and the rest of the campaign brain trust, but it was too quiet and tense up there. I preferred being down in the ballroom, where a large crowd of supporters, most of them barely old enough to vote, was having a good time. The hit of the night was "Bye Bye Boschwitz," sung to the tune of "Bye Bye Blackbird."

Frankly, I didn't know if Boschwitz was going bye-bye or not. The race was closer than it ever had any right to be, and as the evening lengthened, more and more people jammed the party. As the clock passed 11:00 p.m. and headed for midnight, Wellstone's race was still a nailbiter.

I went back up to Paul's suite to see what I could find out. It looked promising, but none of the networks had been bold enough to call a winner. Finally Boschwitz came on TV not to claim victory, not to concede, but to say he was tired and he was going to have a little nip of cognac and then go to bed. Maybe he knew he had already lost; maybe not. But his message was clear: regardless of what the networks decided, there would be no concession coming from Boschwitz's own cognac-coated lips tonight.

By 11:30 there was still no victor, and we began to prepare some "hang-in-there" remarks that Paul could deliver shortly before midnight. There wasn't that much new to say, at least nothing different from what he'd said at 9:00 and 10:00 and 11:00 p.m.—things still look good, thanks to everybody, we ran a good race, nobody thought we'd ever come this far. The crowd was still partying hard, but they were getting restive— they wanted to taste victory, and they wanted to taste it before the bars shut down. They had expected to let loose by 10:00 p.m., then for sure by 11:00. Now it looked like Election Day would come and go for Paul's pent-up supporters without any declared winner.

Just before midnight, we all shuffled onto an elevator for the ride down to the ballroom, Paul and his family, some key campaign staff, and a phalanx of other advisers, party officials, and hangers-on. Paul, whose height meant he had a tendency to be swallowed up in crowds, would need somebody to run interference just to get through the crowd to the stage.

As we walked off the elevator, the pretty and diminutive reporter from the local CBS television affiliate. Amy Marsalis, was fumbling with her mike and her earpiece. She was having trouble hearing what her producer was saying. Suddenly she pushed her way through the bodies surrounding Paul and shoved a microphone in front of him. Camera lights snapped on and shone directly into Paul's exhausted-yet-excited face.

"Paul, CBS has just projected that you are the winner." As Amy was finishing her sentence, the same news flashed up on the ballroom screens, along with the live shot of Paul. The room erupted into screams and cheers.

I'd never been through anything like this before. Suddenly

Wellstone 1990

Paul was swept up and onstage with his family and people from the campaign, beaming and yelling and hoarsely delivering one last, heartfelt stump speech. I was off to the side, watching the crowd, which was filled with people laughing and crying and hugging and cheering. You could see it in their faces and feel it in the room, like some sort of positive force. For once, the good guys won.

Fourteen years removed from that moment, it's hard to recall and even harder to describe. So here are some dispatches from the past, postcards from a long, long time ago when what some of us always hoped could happen finally did happen:

A week has passed since last week's stunning general election, and I think my feet just touched ground for the first time yesterday. It's hard to characterize the feeling; it's more than the thrill of knowing I had a hand in making Minnesota history by helping to elect an underfunded idealist named Paul Wellstone to the U.S. Senate. . . . The name for the feeling, I discovered after a few days of analysis, is power. I woke with the feeling the morning after the election, and after comparing stories with friends over the last week, I am convinced. For the first time in our ever-scrutinized baby boomer lives, we really matter. More than any election in the last 20 years, we—the boomers, the yuppies, the cynical Me Generation—went to the polls and registered a significant opinion.

I have to admit, I didn't believe my generation was up to the task. Right up through Election Day, the thirtysomethings in my office were telling the twentysomethings not to get their hopes up. "We've seen candidates like him before," we told a wide-eyed 23-year-old who had spent the last month stuffing envelopes for Well-

21

stone. "Sure, he worked the hardest, he has the strongest ideas, but he won't win. We've been through a lot of these races. In politics, the best guy never wins."

But from some deep well inside of us, the place where we had stuffed all the dreams of lost elections past, we managed to pull out one last hope that this year might be different. When it was, it surprised us. . . . Oh, we knew we had a certain power all right, but up until now it was always measured in terms of the GNP. . . . We bought turbo Saabs and B&O stereo systems and ranch style homes. . . .

I am 33 years old, a bona fide grownup, and I finally have real power. My vote last week proved that I can help shape this country's future, and there's a place for women, children, the middle class, and poor in the picture. If my generation chooses to continue this trend, we may at last see a smidgen of the Great Society take hold. Not even a turbo Saab could match that.

—Holly Mullen, *Twin Cities Reader,*
November 12, 1990

Yeah, it's the calm before the war storm, but for the moment, life is sweet. Paul "in Jesse Helms's face" Wellstone is on his way to Washington, and suddenly anything and everything seems possible. The parting of the Red Sea. Water into wine. . . . As a member of the Blank Generation that was duped and disillusioned by two-party politics in the '80s (you, too?), I feel a whole lot like James Brown these days: *GOOD*—like I knew I would. A pal o' mine likened the post-Wellstone vibe to when the 1987 Twins won it all, and you betcha by golly, that's the best parallel I've heard yet to describe this enduring euphoria.

—Jim Walsh, *City Pages,* November 14, 1990

Wellstone 1990

The atmosphere at last Tuesday's election night victory party for Paul Wellstone was one of surreal euphoria. Everyone was happy, but no one could quite believe it. People clapped, whooped, embraced, shook their heads at each other. They shouted "Sen-a-tor Well-stone!" but it was as much a reality test as a victory chant.

Tonight the real strength behind the Wellstone campaign was out in force. In addition to the party liberals, there were homeless advocates, gays and lesbians, labor unionists, disabled activists, civil rights and peace & justice groups, and young people—an incredible number of young people. These were individuals who'd grown accustomed to working hard on causes and walking away with little or nothing to show for it. But tonight they had won. The spotlight of political legitimacy was upon them. And it just didn't seem real.

—William Preston Robertson, *City Pages*,
November 14, 1990

In the final analysis, Boschwitz spent nearly $7 million (not counting party and independent expenditures) and Wellstone spent less than $1.5 million, with only about $500,000 of it going into producing all of his ads and buying the ad space and air time. With the help of the many talented people I was able to dragoon into working for the campaign, we were able to do thirteen different TV spots, over twenty different radio spots, and two newspaper ads.

Our work won a multitude of honors. *USA Today* and *Business Week* named the Wellstone ads among the best of the year. Despite my constant criticism of the political consulting industry, their trade organization, the American Association of Political Consultants, had no choice but to award our work a number of Pollies, their honors for the best ads of the political cycle. The readers of *Campaign,* an election trade magazine, voted our "Looking for Rudy" commercial the best political ad in history, beating Reagan's "Morning in America" ad and eking out a narrow victory over Lyndon Johnson's famous "Daisy" ad from 1964.

The most meaningful award in my estimation was the Grand EFFIE, the award for the year's single most effective marketing and advertising campaign. No political campaign had ever won the award in its long history, and my little company, North Woods Advertising, was the first firm located outside New York or California (and undoubtedly the smallest) to take home the honor.

I was justifiably proud of what we had accomplished. My theories about overcoming a gross spending disparity through creative ads and smarter media strategies had just been proved, in a way that would convince everyone but Election Industry, Inc.

But even the awards paled next to the feeling of empowerment for people in Minnesota who had given up faith in politics. The joyousness was contagious, and it served notice that the big-money politics of Election Industry, Inc. was not all-powerful and could be beaten.

Tale of the Tape

Minnesota 1990 U.S. Senate Democratic Primary

Paul Wellstone (DFL)	65%	(226,306 votes)
Jim Nichols (DFL)	35%	(129,302 votes)

Tale of the Tape

Minnesota 1990 U.S. Senate General Election

Paul Wellstone (DFL)	50.5%	(911,999 votes)
Rudy Boschwitz (R)	47.9%	(864,375 votes)

Political Advertising vs. Real Advertising

"Fast Paced Paul" was unlike any political commercial Minnesotans had ever encountered. In it, Paul Wellstone bounded from place to place, his Harpo Marx hair all askew, looking like anything *but* a candidate for the United States Senate. Wellstone introduced the audience to his wife and family, showed them his house, and blurted out his positions on the environment, health care, education, and labor issues, all in just thirty seconds—he told us—because "I don't have a lot of money, so I'm gonna have to talk fast!"

It was riveting. It was funny. And it was the first political TV commercial the state had seen that didn't drive people away from the television and to the refrigerator or the bathroom. In fact, it was the kind of commercial where people watching TV yelled to others in the house, "Quick! Get in here! That commercial I was telling you about is on!"

I had challenged the writers and art directors working on

the project to figure out a way to make Republican incumbent Senator Rudy Boschwitz's money work against him. We knew we were going to be outspent by as much as eight to one or ten to one, so my strategy was to get out in front of Boschwitz's advertising onslaught and essentially establish the notion that he was trying to buy the election.

It was a jujitsu move—use your opponent's superior weight and strength against him. If we could get on the air early enough and creatively enough, people would pay attention to the relatively few commercials we could afford to run. Then every time a Boschwitz commercial aired, it would serve as proof that he was in fact guilty as charged—trying to buy the election.

"Fast Paced Paul" was a mockery of the millions of ineffective political ads that break the cardinal rule of effective advertising. Rather than make one point in a commercial and make it in a compelling and unforgettable way, most political commercials treat the thirty-second time limit as a race against the clock, a challenge to see just how many issues and policy positions and points of information they can possibly stuff into a commercial before time runs out. It's an asinine form of communications that shows no grasp of how audiences receive and digest information, but you still see it used by Election Industry, Inc. in nearly every election held today.

We shot the ad in a day in early August, and had a rough cut of the commercial assembled by the middle of the month. We thought it was hilarious and riveting. Totally unexpected by the voters and by the opposition, it would single-handedly change the way Wellstone was perceived by the public. We couldn't wait to show it to the campaign.

But when Paul and his chief strategist Pat Forciea watched it at the edit studio, they didn't see the same thing we did. At first they thought we were joking, that this was a set-up for the real commercial we would now surely show them instead. We were equally aghast. How could they not recognize that this was one of the most attention-getting political ads ever produced?

When Paul and Pat realized we were serious, that indeed we were recommending they put this on the air, they were speechless. It was the quietest room I've ever been in. Our revolutionary, brilliant commercial was being received with the same facial expressions you'd see on a person reaching into his pocket and unexpectedly finding a dog turd in it.

They left the studio in a shocked silence, both of their faces still frozen in what I now call the unexpected dog turd look. The next day I got a call from Pat telling me not to proceed with finishing any of our other spots.

After we finished editing "Fast Paced Paul," there was nothing for us to do. We were *persona non grata* with the campaign—nobody was even inviting us anymore to those meetings I would generally not attend anyway. Meanwhile, the campaign continued to dither away. This one was beginning to smell like a loser, and my idea of redefining political advertising had seemed to come crashing full tilt into a brick wall.

Then one day Paul was out of town, and—whether by mistake or by unauthorized design—"Fast Paced Paul" somehow got on the air.

The campaign manager claimed he okayed it. The chief strategist for the campaign said he put it on the air, because the Wellstone campaign—a prohibitive favorite to win the Democratic primary—was failing miserably and had nothing left to lose. Another staff person told me the tape went to the stations by mistake.

However it got there, the reaction was instantaneous. "When it ran, BOOM! The phones went off," recalled Pat Forciea after the election. "It had the impact of a knockout punch." Forciea reported that people were saying it was not just the best political ad they had seen, it was the best ad they had ever seen, period. Contributions started to flow into the campaign. Paul Wellstone was suddenly in a place where everybody knew his name. He was drawing crowds and drawing interest. The ranks of campaign volunteers swelled, and they finally felt like they were doing something with a purpose, something important.

The *coup de grace* took place as Paul was returning from a none-too-successful fundraising trip to Washington. A Minnesotan coming off the turnaround flight that Paul was about to board back to Minnesota saw Paul and wrote out a check for $100 on the spot. "I saw your ad on TV last night," he said. "Give 'em hell!"

Paul looked with amazement at the money-in-hand. "What ad did we have on TV last night?" he asked.

Paul's fourth and final campaign manager described it as nothing less than "the turning point of the campaign," adding that "the more we played it, the more we got a positive response." Now the campaign was willing to listen to us and give our work a chance to succeed or fail on its own merits. They were beginning to see that something that didn't look or sound like a political ad was, in fact, a pretty good political ad.

Let's face it: most political ads are crap. If Coke or Pepsi were advertised as badly as most candidates are, we would never drink cola.

Beginning in the mid-1980s, after nearly ten years in commercial advertising, I began to ask myself why this was so.

Like millions of other people, I was aggravated by political ads. While many of us in the commercial world were trying hard to make advertising a more interesting part of the popular culture, political ads were stuck in the worst techniques of the 1940s and 1950s. Political ads had no charm or art to them. You will find a number of people today who believe that the commercials are better than the programs on TV but—

unless they've seen one of our campaigns—you've probably never heard someone say the best thing about election season is the political ads.

You might be surprised to learn that most ad agencies refuse to do political ads. Political campaigns, because of their "here today, gone tomorrow" nature, can't buy advertising time or space on credit from TV and radio stations, or newspapers, or billboard companies the way ad agencies can for their commercial clients. All major media require cash up front for political advertising purchases. Political campaigns are notorious for not paying their bills, leaving both the ad agencies that create their ads and the media that carry their ads holding the bag.

There are other problems, as well. Political campaigns rarely have anyone on staff who understands modern communications and methods of persuasion. Campaign managers become campaign managers not because they understand advertising and communications, but because they know how to organize an office and a volunteer organization. Candidates who come from a business background—rather than a law background or a career in the public sector—may have some sense of this, but few of them come from the marketing or communications departments of their businesses.

Political campaigns operate on shorter time frames, tighter production budgets, and generally with much less strategic planning than commercial ad campaigns. And politics is always a contentious subject, both inside an ad agency and with the agency's clients. So the best ad agencies in the country decided long ago they don't need the hassle, leaving the field open for the charlatans of Election Industry, Inc.

The more I asked why political advertising was so bad, the more frequently I encountered the same defense, parroted by consultant after consultant: "You can't sell candidates the way you sell soap." This was typical of the defensive posturing and the obfuscation that defines Election Industry, Inc. Political media consultants justify the poor quality of their work by insisting that political communications is different from any other sort of marketing or persuasion, and governed by some arcane set of special rules that apply only to politics.

Nonsense. The goal of any communication is, first, to get the audience's attention; second, to impart the information you wish to communicate in a way the audience can comprehend and will accept; and third, to motivate and elicit the desired response from the audience. Looking at it with the benefit of everything I had learned about consumer advertising, I soon discovered that political advertising was failing in nearly every aspect of effective persuasion.

☆ ☆ ☆

Getting Attention

Political ads fall miserably short of this goal, especially compared with product advertising. Product advertising recognizes that it exists in an extremely cluttered media environment and must compete against all other ads and against all other stimuli for the audience's attention.

Political consultants have yet to apprehend this fact, believing instead that audiences compartmentalize advertising, thereby placing a given candidate's ads in competition only with ads for his opponent. But the marketing world's years of collective research into the way advertising works, and the purchase decisions that advertisers try to influence, have demonstrated that consumers *do not* compartmentalize ads by category. Detergent ads don't just compete with other detergent ads: every ad competes with every other ad on TV for the viewer's time and attention.

In terms of the most basic goal of getting attention, political ads perform abysmally. They are neither creative nor interesting enough to engage the viewer. And because of political consultants' tendency to imitate each other, over time, individual political ads become even less and less effective. Political consultants try to get around the innate ineffectiveness of any given ad by making the advertising ubiquitous and unavoidable—a strategy as futile as it is expensive, and a main reason why campaigns today are so costly.

Political ads are also hampered in their ability to get attention by poor production values. Because bad political ads require an inordinate amount of media dollars to even begin to be noticed—and because so few of them work that consultants are usually urging candidates to try other, different ads—little money is spent by the consultants of Election Industry, Inc. on the production of the ads. This then telegraphs to the audience, which is used to seeing more elaborate productions from Pepsi or McDonald's or Ford, that the commercial is a political ad and will therefore be dull and not worth their time or attention. Political ads dig their own grave, and then jump right into it. They have become their own self-fulfilling prophecies.

While the national product ads they're competing with have production costs that now average over $350,000, nearly every political commercial falls into a cost range of between $12,000 and $60,000. So you won't be surprised to learn that Election Industry, Inc.'s political consultants make their money not from the effectiveness of the ads or by producing good ads, but from purchases of ad time, on which they get a commission, usually a healthy 15 percent.

Consequently, campaigns and candidates are regularly paying Election Industry, Inc. to produce political advertising that is so ineffective and inefficient that it requires numerous repeated airings just to be noticed by the voters, who revile it once it's brought to their attention, and then are subjected to it again and again. This makes no sense. There is no return on investment.

You cannot annoy someone into voting for your candidate.

Getting Across the Information

Political ads do a lousy job of this, too. It's not for lack of subject matter—most political ads try to cram as much information about as many issues as they possibly can into thirty seconds. Election Industry, Inc. has candidates talking, announcers announcing, type flying all over the screen, scads of (often phony) newspaper headlines and footnoted sources— all of it in a badly overdone attempt to look authoritative and credible.

Somehow, political consultants have not managed to comprehend one of the most basic rules of modern advertising and persuasion: each communication should have one specific point that the viewer or reader or listener can take away from it. Instead, they pack a commercial wall-to-wall with all kinds of information, in the hope that maybe one of these points might stick. This "everything plus the kitchen sink" approach undermines their very attempts to look more credible and authoritative. All the type crawling across the screen, underlining of type, newspaper graphics, and sources cited only serve to make the viewer more suspicious. It's as if they "doth protest too much."

And most of the information in the ads is of no use to the viewer. Political ads never complete the thought to let people know *why* something is (or should be) important to them. They are stuck on advertising *features* instead of benefits. But features aren't important to consumers, or to voters. *Benefits* are.

The most succinct explanation of the difference between

features and benefits that I ever heard came from a creative director whose agency had just picked up the Sears account:

> "People don't buy polished carbide high-speed quarter-inch drill bits because they want quarter-inch drill bits. People buy quarter-inch drill bits because they want quarter-inch *holes.*"

It's the same in politics. Don't tell me how a candidate has voted, or how many bills he or she has passed, or the fact that he or she has never missed a vote, or his or her position on an issue. Like "polished carbide" and "high speed" and "quarter-inch," those are all features. Give me some *benefits.* Tell me how a candidate's vote or position on an issue made my day-to-day life better. Tell me that my taxes were lowered or my schools were made better or that crime was reduced as a result of this vote or position. Complete the thought. Complete the circle.

☆ ☆ ☆

Motivate the Audience and Elicit a Response

Most political communication is a one-way street: some politician telling you what he wants you to hear. But communication does not really exist unless it goes two ways: you say something to me you think I'd like to know; I acknowledge that I've heard it and I understand it. Only then can you be sure that I've received the message. And only if I have received and understood the message can I respond to it, or take action on it.

The best way I know to make sure that communication is going both ways is to think of every ad as a transaction. You give me thirty seconds of your valuable time; I have to give you something back that you consider valuable. If I fail to do this, you will come away believing I wasted your time, and you will be that much less willing to give me thirty seconds of your attention next time.

What can I give you that will make you feel the transaction is worthwhile? I could touch you emotionally. I could make you see something in a way you've never seen it before (a way you consider valuable). I could give you a new piece of information—information that *you,* not me, consider to be valuable. I could show you a demonstration of something you've never seen before. I could entertain you. I could make you laugh.

One of our ads for the Wellstone campaign was a worthwhile enough transaction that we could successfully keep the viewer's attention for two minutes, an unheard-of length in television advertising.

The Wellstone campaign had been pestering Boschwitz's camp to agree to a series of debates, and getting absolutely no response. This is typical—incumbents generally adopt a "Rose Garden" strategy, preferring not even to recognize their opponent, especially if that opponent is little known and underfunded. (A "Rose Garden" strategy is a trickle-down tactic used by sitting presidents, who often stage media events amid the trappings of the presidency, knowing that it allows them to control the agenda and that it enhances their image of leadership and credibility.)

With this in mind, I decided that since Boschwitz would do everything he could to avoid a debate, we would bring the debate to him. We would follow Paul around with a camera and a sound crew, *60 Minutes* style, as Paul searched for Rudy. If we found him, we would stage a debate, then and there.

So the day after we filmed the scenes for "Fast Paced Paul," I went back out in the Twin Cities with a skeleton camera crew in search of the elusive Boschwitz. The totally unscripted, improvisational, documentary footage we shot that day would eventually become the raw material for "Looking for Rudy," a concept dreamed up by my former art director partner, Bob Barrie, and copywriter Jarl Olsen, and which was inspired by Michael Moore's pursuit of General Motors chairman Roger Smith in his classic documentary *Roger & Me.*

The problem was finding him. We picked a day when we knew Boschwitz was in town from Washington. And we fully intended to find him—after all, we were paying a lot of money (well, a lot of money for *us*) for a film crew to follow us all day. But the comical thing was that we couldn't find Minnesota's United States senator, and nobody seemed to have any idea where he was. First we went to his campaign headquarters in Minneapolis. He wasn't there. They suggested we go to his Senate office in St. Paul, so we drove over there. No Rudy. We went to his place of business, the Plywood Minnesota office. They told us they thought he had flown to Milwaukee on business that day.

I wanted to go to his house, but Paul felt it was going too far to storm his residence in the ritzy Minneapolis suburb of Plymouth, so instead we went back to Paul's campaign headquarters and filmed Paul trying to call Rudy at home. By the end of the day we had covered a lot of miles in a quixotic and somewhat existential attempt to talk to our United States senator. But nobody could find him.

By the time we were finished, I wasn't sure if we could make anything out of the footage. But it didn't matter, because after viewing the rough cut of "Fast Paced Paul," Wellstone and his campaign handlers pulled the plug on "Looking for Rudy." And by the time "Fast Paced Paul" pulled the campaign's bacon out of the fire and delivered the primary to Paul, Boschwitz had preempted the issue, agreeing to meet for three debates.

But once again the problem was finding him; every time Paul's campaign would call Boschwitz's people to work out a schedule for the debates, they would get stonewalled. His strategy was still to ignore Wellstone as long as possible, and to wait until sometime in late October to schedule the debates. We needed those debates earlier, though, and the campaign finally decided to turn us loose and use "Looking for Rudy" to force the Boschwitz campaign to stop stalling and to schedule the debates.

Because of cash flow, we had barely enough money to edit the footage into a commercial and put it on the air; after paying for the edit and a very small media buy, the campaign would be broke. I was down with the flu, so I was uninvolved with the edit until I heard from the writer, Jarl Olsen, that we had a rough cut that was good—though a little long.

A *little* long? When I got to the edit suite, "Looking for Rudy" was a full two minutes in length—ninety seconds longer than the standard television ad. But it was unlike any commercial I had ever seen, more like a mini-documentary, masterfully captured by director-cameraman Greg Cummins. Everyone who had tried to shorten it said that there was no other way of doing it, and after trying it repeatedly myself, I realized they were right. It would be a blockbuster of a commercial. I just had no idea if we could get it on the air— whether stations would even accept a two-minute spot, or whether the campaign could afford to air it enough times to make sure people saw it.

But I also realized that if we could turn "Looking for Rudy" into a news story in its own right, the commercial would be effective no matter how little it ran. It was destined to be the campaign's last stand, though; after crunching the media numbers, I realized we had enough money to run the two-minute commercial exactly *once*. After that, the campaign was flat broke.

Political Advertising vs. Real Advertising

A crapshoot had better odds than this, but somehow I talked the campaign into running the two-minute ad. By tipping the Twin Cities news stations in advance that we had a new two-minute ad, we immediately piqued the interest of the political reporters, all of whom received videocassette dubs of the spot. Normally, any advance copies of a commercial are placed under embargo, holding stations from airing it until the spot has its first paid broadcast. Not this time. I wanted the reporters to watch it and fall in love with it. (Of course, I didn't go out of my way to tell anyone that we only had enough money to run the thing once.)

To everyone's surprise, not least my own, our strategy worked perfectly. "Looking for Rudy" was a lead news story on both the six o'clock and ten o'clock news, on every station. It was turning into a sensation before the ad even ran. Two of the stations played nearly the entire two minutes of the commercial (like us, they realized the storyline made it impossible to shorten or excerpt).

The next morning's papers carried stories about the ad, as they would for nearly a week. News stations aired the spot more the next day. It was water-cooler talk all around the state, at least the 80 percent of the state reached by Twin Cities TV stations and news media.

Most importantly, the campaign got a call from Boschwitz's people the next morning. They were scared to death at all the interest the ad had generated; recognizing the need to end this news story as quickly as possible, they agreed to have a final schedule for all three debates no later than the next afternoon if we agreed not to air the ad anymore.

We agreed. We had to.

We were broke.

Many of us in the advertising world learned long ago the value of entertaining our viewers, but political consultants are still trying to figure it out. I believe most political communications remain stuck in advertising strategies that have been long out-moded and abandoned. One of these strategies dates back to the 1950s: the Unique Selling Proposition theory, which held that a unique advertising claim ("Anacin relieves headache pain faster than any other pain reliever") repeated enough times would convince people of its truth. You might still recall some of those old sixty-second black-and-white commercials. We'd see a tight shot of a woman's head, and she would be gri-macing and rubbing her temples. Then we'd see inside her head, which was an unholy mess of *Sturm und Drang:* light-ning bolts flashing, hammers hitting anvils, tissues pulsing and throbbing. In the meantime, an announcer was yelling at you incessantly, telling you that Anacin could get rid of your headache faster than any other brand. (In fact, if you didn't have a headache before you saw the commercial, you probably had one by the time it was over.)

But painful communications like these depend on a cap-tive audience to succeed. When television was new and people had only three or four channels to choose from (and no re-mote control), a selling approach like this might work. Still, nobody likes to have an unpleasant experience, and most peo-ple will gladly go out of their way to avoid one. Use this ap-proach today, as many political ads do, and your audience is gone at the press of a button.

Another obsolete advertising strategy still favored by Elec-tion Industry, Inc. is advertising recall, the holy grail of the 1970s. In those recession-plagued years, advertisers were look-ing for proof that their advertising expenditures were worth-while. Assuming that a consumer who could readily recall a brand name and some features or attributes of that brand was more likely to buy it, advertisers tested their ads for recall of those attributes, ultimately producing only those ads where lab-tested consumers could parrot back the brand name and some copy points. Political consultants today still very much believe in this technique—a candidate's name awareness or name identification is a critical measuring stick for electability. But this is an oversimplification of the process by which people choose products and candidates—the candidate with the highest name recognition does not always win. (Not to mention that low name identification is the easiest communication hurdle to overcome in politics).

Back in the 1970s, research firms would even test finished commercials with small, representative groups of consumers to see which ads fared best on copy testing scales—tests of viewers' ability to play back attributes they had just heard. The problem was, ads that fared best in the research weren't the same ads that succeeded in getting an audience or selling the product. Often, ads that did well in copy testing do a poor job of motivating the buyer or of instilling desire. Worst of all, copy testing led to ads that telegraphed they were ads. Because so many ads appeared in the same unchanging format, consumers rapidly learned two things: (a) I am watching an ad, and (b) nothing interesting is going to happen for the next thirty seconds.

If communications like this get a response from the audience at all, it is most likely to tune it out or turn it off.

Our final ad for Wellstone was a harrowing experience: conceived, shot, and aired on the same day—the Sunday before Election Day, after we had learned that the Boschwitz campaign had sent out a letter a few days earlier. It was over Rudy's trademark signature, alongside a hand-drawn smiley face. But it was anything but friendly.

"To Our Friends in the Minnesota Jewish Community," read the salutation. After reminding readers that both candidates were "born as Jews," and referring to Boschwitz as the "Rabbi of the Senate," the letter presented a dimmer view of

Wellstone. Claiming he had "no connection whatsoever with the Jewish community or our communal life," it proceeded to criticize Wellstone's child-raising decisions and to align him firmly with Jesse Jackson—and, by extension, Yasir Arafat and Louis Farrakhan.

Last-minute, below-the-belt attacks via direct mail are a stock-in-trade of Election Industry, Inc. But the Jewish vote in Minnesota is minuscule. This reeked more of a complete smackdown; Boschwitz was going to leave no stone unturned with his relentless attacks. He wanted to crush Paul and send a message to interlopers everywhere on behalf of Election Industry, Inc. If some pissant-leftist-hustler/Abbie-Hoffman-lookalike/self-promoting little fake was going to crash the world's most exclusive club, it wasn't going to be on Rudy Boschwitz's watch or at his expense.

The Wellstone campaign called a press conference for the Sunday afternoon before Election Day. Flanked by former Vice President and U.S. Senator Walter Mondale, a bedraggled Paul Wellstone got right to the heart of the matter. "Senator Boschwitz is criticizing me for marrying a Christian and for the way my wife and I have decided to raise our children."

That was the key to our response. Minnesota is one of the most socially liberal states in the nation. Who you decide to marry is strictly your business. How a mother and father choose to raise their children is nobody's business but their own. Not many people in Minnesota would be affected if you told them they weren't very good Jews. But everyone in Minnesota would be outraged if you criticized their choice of their spouse or how they chose to raise their kids.

The press conference ended around 2:00 p.m. It was a strong response, but I had a sinking sensation that it wasn't nearly enough. Unless we did something more, Boschwitz was going to win. There was a Vikings game that night on cable TV, where we had bought as much time as we could afford. It was the perfect opportunity to air a response commercial. But we had no response ad. We also had no ideas, no footage, no studio, and no talent. How could we make a commercial on a Sunday afternoon?

By the time I reached a production studio that agreed to open up for us, I had the inklings of a possible concept. Since Friday, when news of the letter first came out, the press had been haranguing the Boschwitz campaign over it. I remembered seeing a number of negative headlines and reviews associated with Boschwitz's ads, as well as some political cartoons. I asked some of the campaign staff to round up all the papers from around the state with negative stories or headlines or cartoons about Boschwitz and to bring them to the studio, along with some originals of the actual letter.

When the newspapers arrived, I busied the camera operator with shooting all the headlines and cartoons and articles we could find, with zooms and pans and in every imaginable framing. We could make something for the body of the commercial out of this, I thought, but we still had to tie in the Boschwitz letter. And the spot needed a strong visual ending.

When the actual Boschwitz letter showed up, my eye kept coming back to the signature centered on the bottom, the friendly, first-name-only "Rudy" signature with the smiley face drawn next to it. What a fraud, I thought to myself. He'll do anything to save his seat. If we couldn't figure out a way to make him pay for all this, Election Industry, Inc. and its dirty tricks were going to win again.

Maybe it was the smiley face. Or maybe it was the bright green stripe that set off the blue "People for Boschwitz" type on the letterhead. Suddenly I had it. "Mr. Yuck. He's no smiley face. He's Mr. Yuck."

Mr. Yuck is a neon green safety sticker that public health organizations dreamed up to signal young children who can't yet read that something is poison. It looks similar to the ubiquitous bright yellow smiley face, except it's green and it has a frowning face with a downturned mouth and a tongue sticking out. Parents put the stickers on household cleaning products or anything in bottles that kids aren't supposed to drink or taste. Every parent and child in the state would recognize it immediately.

I asked if anyone knew where we could find some stickers. One of the campaign publicists thought he had some at home, under the sink. I asked him to get me as many as he could, in the best condition he could find.

The visual sequence was beginning to take shape in my head. Now we needed the words. I turned my attention back to writing the script while all the rest of this was going on.

I was as worn-out and angry as everyone else. But even I was surprised at the bile and bite in the words that poured out of me, words that eventually said:

Just when voters thought campaigns couldn't get any worse, Rudy Boschwitz proved us wrong. He's aired commercials on Medicare and taxes that have been called "possibly the most misleading political ads to air in the state this year." And now Boschwitz has made an issue out of the fact that Paul Wellstone's wife is a Christian and that his children were brought up as non-Jews. Obviously, Rudy Boschwitz will say or do anything to save his ass. But he's making a lot of Minnesotans sick. Vote for Paul Wellstone.

I started to cut together the visuals. Pans of headlines, cross fades to cartoons, superimpositions of headlines over the now infamous letter. We had called in one of our voice-over announcers, Harlan Saperstein, who quickly jumped into the recording booth. I knew the station would never let us say the word "ass" in the commercial, so we changed it to "seat," and

Harlan delivered the line in such a way that there was no doubt what we really meant to say.

When the Mr. Yuck stickers arrived, they looked like they had been under the sink for a long time. There were two of them that were presentable enough to use in the spot. And we had only two original copies of the Boschwitz letter. That meant just two takes of a hand placing Mr. Yuck over the Boschwitz smiley face, because the stickers would ruin the letter if we tried to remove them.

I looked around. "OK, who wants to be the hand model?" I asked. "No pressure. But we only have two chances to get this right."

Everyone was in agreement that I should stop directing and do it myself. I couldn't. My hands were shaking. We now had less than an hour to finish shooting, edit and slate the commercial, and get it out the door to the station. I can't remember who finally accepted the challenge. Neither one of the takes was perfect, but they would have to do.

By 5:45 p.m. we had something assembled. It was time for the finishing touches to be put on the spot, to duplicate it, and get it into a car and on its way to the stations. It was not the best ad I had ever done, by any stretch of the imagination. But it was undoubtedly the fastest. And, as it would turn out, one of the most effective.

The editor looked at me and said we needed a title for the commercial.

I thought for a second, then a slow smile came over my face. "Bunch of Boschwitz," I said. "We're calling this spot 'Bunch of Boschwitz.'"

We still weren't done. We got dubs of the ad to all four TV news desks, with word that it would be on the Vikings game that night. It was a lead story on every single 10:00 p.m. newscast.

All through the next day, Monday, the news was filled with

talk about the Jewish letter. Boschwitz's dirty trick had back-fired. People were outraged, especially Jews, and Boschwitz paid for it in the voting booth the next day, and in the press, which continued to criticize his campaign in postmortems.

Our ad did what we needed it to do. But too much political advertising is too similar to Boschwitz's attack letter, filled with toxic content. Too often, the formulaic, often negative political ads of Election Industry, Inc. have an even more toxic effect: they inspire people to choose not to vote, thereby turning the reins of our entire democratic process over to a highly motivated minority.

It might be a stretch to say that bad ads equal bad government, but it's probably not as much of a stretch as you might think.

Effective Political Campaigning

I have been persuading the public of one thing or another for over twenty-five years now. And I've learned that whether you are selling a service, a product—or whether you are a candidate selling yourself—there is a ladder of persuasion that you have to climb.

☆ ☆ ☆
Credibility

The first step for any campaign is credibility. Credibility is a rare enough commodity in politics, but it is the absolute foundation every upset victory is built upon.

People have to believe you. If they don't, you'll have a hard time—and a very, very *expensive* time—trying to convince them to vote for you or your candidate. What's more, it's impossible to get better-than-average voter turnout if people don't or won't believe your candidate. When voters feel like they can't believe *any* of the candidates, it leads to a race-to-the-bottom, "lesser evil" type of campaign, which is hardly inspiring, and results in low turnout elections.

Credibility is something the candidate either establishes with people, or not. There is very little middle ground. People want to vote for candidates they can trust. And no voter will ever trust a candidate until that candidate first establishes credibility with the voter.

☆ ☆ ☆

Legitimacy

Legitimacy is something that is often out of the control of the candidate. Oddly, while credibility can be established by the candidate, legitimacy usually can't. Legitimacy is something that is conferred upon a campaign by people outside the campaign—the press, observers, and most importantly, the voters. And legitimacy has more to do with the campaign than the candidate. The litmus tests for legitimacy are the ability to organize a working campaign, to have a functional campaign structure and operation, to be able to attract a critical mass of financial support (in a presidential race, measured in millions, not less), and to be able to recruit committed volunteers.

There are more practical, specific ways in which legitimacy is demonstrated, such as the capability to get on the ballot—which in many states has been made extremely difficult for independent or third-party candidates by our two-party duopoly and by the incumbents—controlled by Election Industry, Inc.—who make the ballot access rules.

Of course, the most visible demonstration of legitimacy also happens to be the method most favored by the media who both bestow it and profit from it: the ability and willingness to invest in advertising. Nothing seems to establish a candidate's legitimacy faster than a high-profile ad campaign, preferably on television.

In fact, due to the wanton ad expenditures that go on in statewide and national elections, many in the media have been preconditioned to believe a candidate is not legitimate unless his or her campaign is on TV. Newspaper advertising has been disregarded now for decades by Election Industry, Inc. and by the media (even newspaper reporters!). Radio advertising is traveling down the same path. TV has rapidly become the only game in town for demonstrating a candidate's legitimacy—advertising dollars which eventually end up in the pockets of the very same media conglomerates that award legitimacy to the candidates. Nice system, eh?

The legitimacy rung is set higher for some candidates. Third-party and independent candidates are scrutinized much more closely than the profligate-spending campaigns of major-party candidates. The media regularly puts third-party or independent candidates under a microscope: they must constantly continue to prove the legitimacy of their campaigns. Every mistake and misstep becomes magnified for these underfunded challenger campaigns, because it opens the door for the press to question the campaign's or the candidate's competence.

(If a third-party campaign has a major travel or transportation snafu, for example, every inconvenienced member of the press corps will start bleating about "How is this person going to be capable of running a government when he can't even run his own car pool?"—and that's assuming the campaign has gotten to the point where it receives press coverage.)

This attitude has a damning and diminishing effect on independent and third-party candidates (and even under-

dog major-party candidates) that most Republicans and Democrats rarely have to contend with. For example, while many
people agree that Michael Dukakis, Bob Dole, and Al Gore ran
awful campaigns, nobody would say they weren't legitimate
candidates. But an independent candidate would be barbe-
cued by the press at every opportunity if he or she ran the kind
of campaign Dukakis, Dole, and Gore ran. (Which, thankfully,
most independent candidates can't do, because they don't
have enough money to hire the legions of advisers and
fundraisers and pollsters and staffers and consultants who
royally screw up these big campaigns.)

And what the media giveth, the media can take away. For
no matter how well a third-party or independent campaign is
doing, the legitimacy question comes up again near the finish
line. The press wonders why they should spend any time covering a campaign that can't win, and writes about that. The
major-party candidates echo the same thing, and tell the voters that they'll be wasting their vote if they vote on the basis of
the best candidate, as opposed to who's better between the Republican and the Democrat. And the voters read and hear all
this, and begin to wonder if they are chumps for voting for the
person who they think in their heart of hearts is the best person for the job.

People want to believe in their vote, and—rightly or
wrongly—people do buy into a "wasted vote" argument. Successful campaigns convince people they have a legitimate
chance at winning, whatever the odds.

Most political consultants, political scientists, and political
opinion makers—even Election Industry, Inc.—wouldn't disagree with me up to this point. But they believe once you
have established credibility and legitimacy, you can move on
to talking about issues or policies or the deficiencies of your
opponent.

I don't.

I think you need to ascend another rung of the ladder first, and that is . . .

☆ ☆ ☆
Likeability

I have been touting the importance of likeability as a necessary component of effective political campaigns for over a dozen years now. Yet it tends to get written off as unmeasurable and therefore less important by the pollsters, political scientists, and other pooh-poohing poobahs of Election Industry, Inc.

Why this is so hard to comprehend, I don't know. Ronald Reagan, Bill Clinton, and George W. Bush were all elected president in spite of perceived major deficiencies, just because of their charm and rapport with voters. Bob Dole's campaign for president in 1996 was a complete disaster because his handlers turned a war hero with a distinguished record in Congress—and a guy who everyone agrees is pretty nice and funny—into everyone's mean uncle.

Possibly the most intriguing example of this is Clinton. There should be no doubt in anyone's mind that if Bill Clinton could have run for a third term, despite all his lies and missteps, he would have easily won reelection.

Among certain groups of people—particularly women and African American voters—Clinton's likeability is so strong that it trumps his well-established problems with credibility. Bill Clinton can be lying to you, you know he's lying to you, he knows *you* know he's lying to you, you know *he* knows you know he's lying to you, yet you still choose to believe him or at least overlook the lie.

As Senator Bob Kerrey of Nebraska famously observed, "Bill Clinton is an unusually good liar."

That is a unique . . . *something* (I hesitate to call it a skill, but I guess it is) in politics.

Here's why likeability is important. Voters have to feel comfortable having you the candidate in their living room, especially in these days of TV-oriented campaigns. If they're not—if they can't trust you and don't like you—it doesn't matter what you have to say about social security or education or foreign policy or any of the Big Issues. They aren't listening.

You can have the best ideas in the world, but if voters don't like you, they aren't going to vote for you. They can either get with you, or they can't. And if they can't, you are not going to step up to the final rung of the ladder, which is . . .

Preference

If you've moved up the ladder this far, voters now have to look at you in the context of other candidates and choose who they are going to spend their vote on. If they don't trust you, if they don't think you are competent to do the job, if they don't believe you have a chance to win, and if they don't like you, guess what?

It's not going to be you.

So how do you achieve preference? Read on.

The Unbearable Dumbness
of Polling

In my many years in politics, I have come to learn that there are two phrases that, joined together, should make every candidate turn and run: "I'm a pollster" and "I'm from Washington and I'm here to help." I didn't know this yet in 1990, but I was about to find out.

Just after Paul Wellstone won his primary in 1990, I found myself sitting in another typically overpopulated strategy meeting with a Democratic Party operative from Virginia. He knew exactly what Paul should do, based on what Doug Wilder had done when running for governor of Virginia in 1988. Because it had worked for Wilder in Virginia, he was convinced it would work for Wellstone in Minnesota.

I explained to him that I saw a few flaws in his thinking, namely: this was 1990, not 1988. Doug Wilder was a black man running for governor in a southern state, Paul Wellstone a transplanted Jew from North Carolina running for the U.S. Senate in a state just south of Canada.

Aside from that, I said, you probably got everything right.

He was on the next plane back to D.C.

No wonder pollsters hate me.

Of all the Election Industry, Inc. types who insinuate themselves into political campaigns, pollsters are the worst. Nearly every campaign that has jumped the track and gone seriously off course can trace the cause back to a poll that was fatally flawed but defended to the death by its pollster.

Pollsters see themselves as oracles. Their relationship to candidates is like the ancient seers, who would cut open a bird, read its entrails, then tell fortunes or predict the future. (But if pollsters get the future wrong, they'll hide behind the excuse that a poll is a "snapshot in time," not a predictor of future events, despite the fact that for decades they have sold their wares as a predictive device and as a means to formulate strategy for countless campaigns.)

Polling in politics is equivalent to marketing research in the world of commerce. Yet pollsters regularly get away with things that would get them defenestrated in any semicompetent American business.

In marketing research, we hire an independent, third-party company to formulate a research study, execute it, and tabulate the results. We tell them what we want to find out and from whom, make sure questions are scrubbed clean of any possible bias, then step aside to let them complete their work.

Pollster work differently. Whether they are qualified or not, they immediately attempt to install themselves as key strategists, getting involved in deciding what the campaign wants or needs to find out, who should be asked, and how the questionnaire should read.

Pollsters are the not-so-secret weapons of Election Industry, Inc. With the backing of the two major parties and the parties' campaign committees, pollsters chant the conventional wisdom of Washington, keeping candidates in line with the party platform and under the thumb of the party itself.

In commercial marketing research, the researchers who have conducted the study tabulate the results, come in, present them to you . . . and leave. It is not up to them to interpret the data—after all, what do they know about selling cat food compared to a brand manager or director of marketing who knows the product, knows the customers, and is at a company that has been making and selling cat food for the last hundred years?

This lack of knowledge concerns pollsters not a whit. You may be a congressional candidate who has lived in the district for fifteen years, you may know the people of the district and their problems and concerns intimately; but some Election Industry, Inc. pollster who has never set foot in the district for longer than fifteen minutes will confidently tell you exactly what you need to do to get elected, based on a (usually badly flawed) survey of three hundred people in the district.

And you may disagree, but you do so at your own peril.

Pollsters regularly skew questionnaires to support the party line or the overall party strategy; or to generate the kind of responses the candidate or campaign wants to hear; or to support their own peculiar strategy for the campaign. They then use their compromised findings to tout their own private version of the truth, or what they believe the truth should be, and to hide what is really their own opinion and speculation behind "The Data."

Beware "The Data." They use The Data as a club to beat others into submission. If I had a dollar for every time a pollster would combat my arguments by saying, "Bill, this is not *me* talking, this is The Data," well, I would have an awful lot of dollars.

The reality is, with pollsters often being the least qualified people in a campaign to dictate strategy (I'd rather take my chances with the candidate's friends or spouse) and polls regularly being as inaccurate as they are, it's not hard to figure out why so many political communications efforts are ineffective and why so much money is wasted in campaigns.

Pollsters love to think of themselves as political historians, the war college of elections past. And the political parties see their organizations as keepers of that history. Together, pollsters and political parties are forever insisting that campaigns need to adopt a particular strategy, because that is what worked for so-and-so in such-and-such a year.

This, too, is nonsense. It's why so many campaigns are always fighting the last war.

I liken it to trying to drive your car while constantly looking in the rearview mirror. It's tough to see what's coming when you're always watching your backside.

Political campaigns take place every two years. In the case of presidents and governors, every four years; and in the case of U.S. senators, every six years. Are you exactly the same as you were six years ago, or four years ago, or even two years ago? Haven't things changed for you and your neighbors and family members in that time?

As someone who has spent nearly all of his adult life in the advertising and marketing business, I tell candidates that we are out there persuading the American public 365 days a year, year-in and year-out, all over the country. Pollsters and political consultants do this once every couple of years.

Who do you think has a better grip on the pulse of most Americans?

Pollsters will not tell you their refusal rates: the number of people in any demographic slice who were contacted by the polling firm but who refused to be surveyed.

Why is the refusal rate important? Well, do you know anyone who really enjoys spending twenty minutes out of their day, usually around dinnertime, to talk to a marketing researcher about anything, least of all politics? We know on the marketing research side that the number of people refusing to talk to survey callers is huge and getting larger. Cell phones, caller ID, and Do Not Call lists are making it harder just to find enough people to answer the phone in any demographic slice, much less get them to respond to a twenty-minute battery of questions. Consequently, you should factor the refusal rate among any particular demographic group into the overall result to get a truer picture of the statistical significance of that demographic slice.

In its simplest terms, polling and marketing research works like this: you define a particular universe of people (such as registered voters or people who buy cat food), then break that larger universe into a smaller one (say, Democratic registered voters over the age of thirty who have voted in each of the last three elections, or women who have bought cat food in the last thirty days who are over the age of twenty-five with at least one child and a household income exceeding $50,000). You can also put a geographic qualifier on it (for voters, it might be those in a particular state or district; for cat food buyers, it could be those in a particular metropolitan area or region or even nationally), then you figure out how many people fitting these descriptions exist in the specified area. Once you have a fairly accurate number of the universe of the people you are trying to survey, the research company calculates a much smaller number of people whose opinions can be surveyed and then projected over the group at large, within a statistical margin of error.

Margins of error are, basically, fudge factors. Surveys always have margins of error, noted as "plus or minus" numbers alongside a certain percentile. For example, a survey may have a margin of error of "plus or minus 5 percent at the 95th percentile." In theory, that means if you replicate the survey 100 times, 95 of those surveys would show similar results, with percentages of any given survey within plus or minus 5 percent of the numbers from any of the other 94 of those 95 surveys.

Obviously, the bigger the sample size, the more accurate the results should be. For instance, I consider any statewide survey with a sample size of less than a thousand or twelve hundred respondents to be pretty worthless. (Two to three thousand respondents would be even better, and perhaps even necessary, depending on the population of the state.) But pollsters regularly do statewide surveys of half or one-third this size.

Always look closely at the margin of error and degree of confidence (another fudge factor, shown as a percentage number). Any survey that comes in at lower than the 95th percentile is also pretty worthless, in my mind. At the 90th percentile, you have a one-in-ten chance that the survey is completely wrong. Those might sound like pretty good odds to you, but it's a complete waste of money with the technology available to marketing research today.

The margin of error is the ultimate fudge factor. Even something that sounds as good as "plus or minus 5 percent" really means that there could be a ten point swing in any given result. That is to say, something reported at 50 percent might actually be 55 percent or it might be 45 percent. Again, that may not sound like a lot, but in most two-person elections, 5 percentage points is a pretty big margin, and a 60 to 40 percent differential—10 points moving to either side of 50 percent—is considered a blowout.

Let's return to our previous example. Assume you have a completed survey and the refusal rate was very high. What do you really have? Do you have a statistically significant report on registered Democratic voters over the age of thirty who have voted in the last three elections in California? Do you have a statistically significant report on mothers over the age of twenty-five who have purchased cat food in the last thirty days?

Or do you, in reality, have a survey from a group that likes to take surveys? (And I would suggest to you that people who like to talk to pollsters are not—decidedly not—normal people.)

Ever wonder why issues like social security or prescription drug prices rank so high on the list of voter concerns in most political polls? Well, who do you think is most apt to be at home during dinnertime, most likely to answer the phone, and—sadly—most likely to be alone and grateful for another voice to talk to? Old people.

Another favorite pollster vehicle is the focus group. Pollsters love to use focus groups to support their strategies and points of view, which is exceptionally idiotic, because focus groups consist of ten to twenty-five people and focus group results cannot be quantified or extrapolated in any accurate way.

Focus groups can be useful for gathering general opinions and information and attitudes, but they are best used only as windows into the individual mind-sets of people in a given group rather than as representative of the entire group. A focus group might be valuable at the beginning of a campaign, when you are trying to get insights into particular kinds of voters and how political issues affect their everyday lives.

In this way, focus groups can sometimes help a campaign struggling to find a "message" (although I have found that if a candidate can't tell you clearly and succinctly and honestly why he or she is running, you are going to have a problematic campaign). But focus groups should never be used (as pollsters use them) to evaluate or "approve" specific strategies, messages, or executions—because the opinions are those of individuals and not quantifiable, and they are a waste of money when used that way.

Focus group research can be rife with opportunities for inaccuracy. The small sample size means the likelihood is high of it being completely unrepresentative or misrepresentative of the larger group. As opposed to the problems phone surveys have with refusal rates, focus groups often have problems with the people who *agree* to participate. Too often they are made up of opinionated individuals who like attending these forums to hold forth with their own opinions (or who just like the $25 or $50 and free sandwiches, cookies, and soft drinks they get for participating). Opinionated individuals or regular focus group participants often dominate the conversation and prevent other viewpoints from being expressed. More timid participants or people with an innate desire to please or to get along in a group will often agree with viewpoints previously expressed by others to avoid thinking too hard about the issue, to avoid engendering any controversy, or just to move the proceedings along so they can collect their $50 and get the hell out of there.

Moderators are another biasing factor. Moderators often subtly or not too subtly prejudice the proceedings. Some people in a focus group will flat-out lie, because they dislike the moderator, because they fear the opprobrium of the moderator or the group, because they are not comfortable with their own opinion on the issue, or because they believe they know and dislike who is sponsoring the research.

Or just to be perverse, because they hate the notion of political polling and being measured and prodded. That would be a good enough reason for me.

I don't believe in polling, but I do believe in targeting.

Election Industry, Inc. and other observers of our work tend to credit the creativity of North Woods Advertising's ads as the main reason behind tremendous upsets like Paul Wellstone's in 1990, Jesse Ventura's in 1998, and Denver mayor John Hicken-looper's in 2003. And it's true that our work has revolutionized political advertising and that we do—by far—the most creative and attention-getting political work in the country.

But that's just the tip of the iceberg. Our communica-tion strategies and our media buying have as much to do with the effectiveness of the ads as the ads themselves. And those strategies and media buys are dictated by targeting.

Targeting, in its simplest terms, can be described like this: There is a percentage of any population that is never going to vote for your candidate, no matter what. You can run all the ads you want, make all the promises you can think of, pander better than Al Gore on his best day, and these voters still aren't buying.

Why waste time and money trying to persuade people who can't be persuaded?

On the other hand, there is a percentage of the voting pop-ulation that will always vote for your candidate, no matter what. Your candidate could be caught in bed multiple times—with multiple sheep—and some people will still vote for him.

Especially if you are running a campaign with limited re-sources, why spend a lot of time talking to these people?

Money spent continuing to convince the already con-vinced is money wasted. This is one of the biggest fallacies of Election Industry, Inc. They believe in "solidifying your base," and most campaigns spend far too much time and money on this. I always ask the obvious question, "Well, if they need so-lidifying, then they aren't exactly your core supporters, are they?"

The key to every election is the group in the middle—persuadable swing voters. That's the group I want to exert nearly 100 percent of my time and spend nearly 100 percent of my money working to convince.

It sounds logical and simple, but targeting can be damnably hard to do. The best voter targeting is a strange amalgam of statistics, data crunching from past elections, and the kind of intangible gut feeling that tells great archeologists to dig here rather than there. And targeting is as much an art as it is a science, relying as much on having a sense of psychographics and demographics—even anthropology—as on understanding mathematics and statistics and regression analysis (none of the latter are strong suits of mine).

The best targeters are incapable of fully and logically explaining the alchemy behind their recommendations. When they finally arrive at the right solution, they just know it in their gut. The best targeters I have seen are more wizard than scientist—they have an inherent, almost mystical feel for figuring out which data to scrutinize, which data to ignore, and how to weight all the various factors involved.

Research is a necessary precursor to targeting—targeting's raw materials consist of information like voter demographics, and vote counts from previous elections broken down geographically. In developing strategy and deciding who we are really talking to in our races, I first of all like to figure out the gross number of votes my candidate will need to win. This is not a percentage, this is a total number of votes that we are sure will lead to victory. Next we break the voting universe into various subcategories, based on demographical information, psychographical information (such as those who may favor a certain social issue), and geographical location. We figure out the total number of voters in each of these subcategories, factor out any overlaps, then decide what percentage of that audience we can realistically expect to get without spending a lot of time and effort on them. Add up these categories, and you have what most campaigns would consider to be their *base* vote—their core group of supporters.

If your base vote total is greater than the gross number of

votes you need to win, congratulations: you're working for an incumbent, probably in one of the more than 400 elections every two years that aren't considered competitive. (If not, you're either very fortunate or very bad at addition.) But chances are, the base vote alone doesn't get you anywhere near the total number of votes you will need to be assured of a comfortable win.

Next, you must play a game of numbers. You eliminate that portion of the electorate that you are certain will go to your opponents—their base votes. What's left is the true swing vote—the persuadables.

And that's where targeting comes in. Even though all votes are equal—one person, one vote (unless you're in Chicago or Florida or some other strange place)—all persuadables are not. Your candidate will have greater appeal for some swing vote categories—you can expect to persuade a greater percentage of that group. Some groups are larger than others, so getting 2 percent or 10 percent of that subcategory might be more worthwhile than getting 90 percent of all left-handed, red-headed Italian women with 2.5 children and a household income of under $35,000 living in C- and D-sized counties. Some groups will require more time and money to achieve a reasonable percentage; others may be able to be persuaded relatively cheaply.

This is not brain surgery, but it is where almost every campaign is won or lost. (If you get 100 percent of the swing vote and still don't win, then you shouldn't have been running in the first place.)

All these groups need to be worked through and prioritized until you have reached your vote total. The permutations and combinations can be endless, but I've always found it to be a worthwhile exercise.

Meanwhile, the worthlessness of the exercise in futility called polling is more evident now than ever before.

Remember Election Night 2000? It was a polling operation—Voter News Service (VNS), jointly owned by ABC, CBS, NBC, CNN, Fox News, and the Associated Press—that made a complete hash of the presidential election by calling the deciding state of Florida first for Al Gore, then George W. Bush.

After the debacle of 2000, VNS went through a complete overhaul of their methods and systems, determined to have a grossly more efficient methodology in place by the 2002 elections.

In the late afternoon of Election Day 2002—which was a debacle for Democratic pollsters, none of whom saw the Republican blowout coming—VNS contacted all its subscribers to say that the data they were providing with their revamped system was probably not reliable. For many of the reasons I've described above, the service was unable to construct accurate statistical models.

Mark this one down as a battle won by citizens trying to reclaim their democracy from Election Industry, Inc. Confounding pollsters weakens their exalted status in Election Industry, Inc. and may result in candidates who are true leaders, or political parties developing actual ideas rather than regurgitating whatever the pollsters say their audiences want to hear.

But give VNS some credit for honesty. In early 2003, the service announced it was giving up. Let me repeat. The most sophisticated and best funded polling operation in the country, working for the nation's largest media outlets, after more than two years of intense study, said that polling accurately is impossible and closed its doors.

Let's hope it isn't replaced by some other cockamamie crystal ball service courtesy of Election Industry, Inc.

R.I.P., VNS.

People for Perot 1992

Perhaps no one exposed the chinks in the armor of Election Industry, Inc. more effectively than billionaire populist Ross Perot. His 1992 Independent presidential run was a watershed moment in contemporary American politics, in part because he posed a genuine threat to beat Election Industry, Inc. at its own game. He did so by utilizing some of its favorite tools to try to control campaigns—money, high-priced political "expertise," media manipulation—as well as some very effective strategies and tactics a traditional campaign would never attempt.

Though most observers missed it at the time, this was never truer than in July 1992, when Perot staged his sudden withdrawal from the presidential race (a race he had yet officially to enter). Under the leadership of an impressively experienced and bipartisan team of advisors, Perot's campaign appeared to self-destruct in a meltdown that even Election Industry, Inc. reliables Democrat Hamilton Jordan (from Jimmy Carter's campaign) and Republican Ed Rollins couldn't prevent. By all appearances, Perot was handing the election back to the major parties (even as he once again stole the media spotlight from their predictable machinations).

I knew better—or at least I realized better one sunny morning in late July, a few weeks after Perot shut down his still-unannounced campaign. "He's not leaving the race," I said to myself, suddenly seeing how he was yet again outmaneuvering his opponents with a move that wasn't even on their radar screens. Perot may not have been of the game, but he seemed to know how to play it. The unorthodox route he had taken to get this far was starting to look ever smarter, revealing weaknesses in the Election Industry, Inc. game plan for those who knew where to look.

The first thing that got me really thinking about how far Ross Perot could go was his money. Like everyone, I had noticed the Perot circus in early 1992, and saw that he was making a funny kind of sense to people. I appreciated his anger at the two-party stranglehold on politics, and I saw some appeal in his idea of a private citizen coming in to clean out the political stables.

My curious interest took a distant backseat to other campaigns with whom we were in contact until April, when the op-ed people at the *New York Times* asked me for an advertising professional's take on the impact a candidate spending $60 million of his money on advertising could have in the election. I had recently noted a report that helped put that question in perspective—namely, that Pepsi had spent $79 million to advertise Pepsi Cola in 1991. Now this wasn't total spending for all Pepsi products, but it was how much PepsiCo spent on its core brand, the second-largest-selling soft drink in

America, over their entire fiscal year. Perot was talking about spending $60 million in what might be little more than a twelve-week period.

Could that have an impact? No more so than the earth colliding with a really large meteor.

The money would be a factor only if it were well spent, of course, and I wrote in the *Times* that I saw two objectives for Perot's largesse: to define himself and his qualifications, and to remind everyone what a sorry state the country was in. With the country looking for a savior, Perot was better off remaining a mythical figure as long as possible; by relying on paid advertising rather than free media, he could maintain control over how his qualifications were perceived by the public. And Perot didn't have to target his competitors with traditional attack advertising, which would have made him one of them: as an independent, his outsider status gave him a unique opportunity to spread a negative, don't-feel-good general message taking advantage of the public's suspicions that their elected representatives weren't telling them how bad things really were.

Shortly after the *Times* piece ran, I received a tentative, indirect contact from the Perot campaign. By this time the Republican political consultant Ed Rollins was already on board, however, and he was in the process of bringing in Hal Riney, the San Francisco adman behind most of the best commercials for Reagan's 1984 reelection. Nothing happened, and several more months would pass before I would hear again from the Perot campaign.

The *Times* piece also led to an NBC *Today* show appearance, as one of a panel of ad people brought in to discuss how they would handle Perot's advertising if given the chance. I roughed out a concept that was true to what I assumed his campaign recognized as the secret of its appeal. I knew his supporters were more dissatisfied with the current state of their government and their politics than they were passionate about one man; he was merely the vessel carrying the message, as well as their hopes and dreams. The ad I described didn't even show Perot—but it did offer a message of empowerment, of telling people something that they desperately wanted to believe, but had heard too often before from so many typical politicians who had eventually let them down.

By this time, Perot's novelty and luster were already beginning to fade with the press, who started to question his capability to be president and his knowledge about many specific issues. In response to this scrutiny, Perot abruptly made the decision to curtail some of his media appearances, in order to take a long enough hiatus to bone up on the issues and generate campaign position papers on them.

This late-spring hiatus was followed in turn by a midsummer meltdown. As the media pressure continued to mount, Perot's paranoia toward the press came closer to the surface, while the political professionals he brought in to run his populist campaign were emerging as problems themselves, rather than part of the solution. In mid-July, he capriciously shut down his independent campaign before he ever formally began it.

I was confused and disappointed—if only because of the excitement Perot was bringing to an otherwise stultifying election—until the July morning it dawned on me that he hadn't really left the race. Rather, Perot had simply regained control of the message and the agenda. Of course, every operative of Election Industry, Inc. wants to control as much of any election agenda as he can get his hands on; the (often illusory) promise of this control is a large part of what they sell their candidate clients. But Perot had ways of achieving this that aren't available to most candidates. His upcoming fall gambit, the network prime time infomercial, would put him back on the map and would be far beyond the resources of even Bill Clinton or George Bush. Perot's idea to simply close up shop for a while was unheard of. Nobody could run for president by constantly jumping in and out of the pool . . . could they?

But Perot either was a shrewd candidate or was getting some pretty shrewd advice. At the time that he shut down his campaign, Perot was under greater and greater scrutiny from the press. The myth of Ross Perot was starting to be investigated more closely, and Ross Perot the man didn't like it. At times he would be visibly perturbed on news programs when an interviewer would press into areas that he didn't want to visit, or wouldn't let him redirect the conversation toward where he wanted it to go.

Perot had actually already succeeded in everything he needed to accomplish by the early summer. Things could only get worse for him through the rest of the summer. So he cut and ran. It was for exactly the same reason as his earlier "hiatus"—to escape the press. But this time, rather than characterizing it as a hiatus, he simply "quit."

What did dropping out do? It meant he was still, officially, not a candidate, and therefore off limits to the press, who figured he was just another flash in the pan, and turned their attention elsewhere. But dropping out also telescoped down the amount of time he would need to run as an official candidate if he reentered the race. He wanted to signal to supporters that he was serious about running early enough for them to do the hard work of getting ballot access, but he didn't want to run a full-length campaign. Most unknown candidates without a political party need all the time—and all the media attention—they can muster before Election Day, to catch the voters' eye and to get their messages out. Candidates who have $100 million of their own money to spend don't.

And if that money was now going to be packed into, say, late August to early November rather than early spring through early November, imagine even how much *more* effective it could be.

So I had already had the revelation by the time Ross Perot got back into the race in August. He hit the airwaves with a blizzard of advertising time—infomercials, the more traditional thirty-second ads, and less traditional sixty-second spots. The ads were somewhat interesting, but not, I thought, very effective.

In fact, despite my initial fascination and trepidation about Perot's advertising budget, in the final analysis advertising didn't have that much to do with Perot's success. His idea of running infomercials was more powerful than the infomercials themselves—hardly anybody could sit through the entire thirty minutes. None of his ads was particularly memorable or different or effective. No one remembered much about Perot's specific plans or policies, but nearly everyone to this day remembers some of his language or his dorky charts. In this case (as the independent movement would see later with Jesse Ventura), the medium wasn't the message. The *messenger* was the message.

But what little success Perot had in his infomercials and advertising was amplified exponentially by the debates. Perot may not have had his custom-built infomercial set and his trusty charts in the debates, but he still had his outsized personality and his way with the language. Perot's lasting legacy will likely be that he did so well in the debates that it forced the two major parties and Election Industry, Inc. to collude to make sure no one outside their carefully controlled system could ever do that well again.

North Woods Advertising was still interested in becoming involved in Perot's rebel assault on the system, but it didn't look like it was going to happen. His campaign had closed ranks, hunkered down, and bunkered up. The grand experiment of pairing Rollins and Jordan was done. Perot's campaign had reverted back to what it wanted to be all along—something insularly Texas, but very far away from the nullibiety (the state of being nowhere) of Election Industry, Inc.

Despite the fact that no one really knew who was in charge from one day to the next, Perot's campaign did awfully well. Perot mostly let his advertising do the talking for him, and in this way could afford to avoid talking to press he didn't think would treat him fairly. It's true that the press would still continue to ask questions and pick him apart and question his capability for the job, but his advertising expenditures and especially the idea of his infomercials reburnished his persona, and did so in a loud enough voice that if it was not drowning out the negative press, it was at least making the voters more hard of hearing.

Less than two weeks before Election Day, as Perot continued to attract disaffected voters, I got a call from Gerry Celente, a family acquaintance who had first contacted me about Perot months earlier. He was calling on behalf of John Jay Hooker, a Nashville millionaire Democrat who I would later learn was perhaps the single most influential person in convincing Perot to run for president.

Though he was not yet identifying Hooker by name, Gerry described a labyrinthine chain of phone calls from Dallas to Nashville to him in upstate New York. Hooker knew that Perot was on the verge of a major breakthrough in American politics, and wanted to hold on to as many of the Perot voters down the stretch as he could. He also wanted to reinforce Perot voters so they would be less likely to crater in the face of a "wasted vote" argument during the final days. Hooker asked Gerry who could accomplish this. Gerry thought I could, and asked if I would be interested in working on a final ad—a "closer," in the parlance of campaigns, for Ross Perot.

To me, it all seemed kinda Twilight Zone. No campaign operates this way, with a phone tree that hopscotches around the country before anybody can make a decision. But then I recalled all the weirdness that had gone on before in this campaign. What the hell, I thought. As my favorite political handicapper Hunter S. Thompson says, "When the going gets weird, the weird turn pro."

Gerry (via Hooker and someone in Dallas, I presume) told me I had the weekend to get some concepts figured out and that I would need to send him something on Monday. He would then send them to Nashville, where they would be reviewed and then passed along to Dallas.

I asked if there was any particular strategy behind this, but they hadn't gotten any further than wanting to minimize the number of votes they were losing over the final days. They were looking for a silver bullet and I guess I was the Lone Ranger. But Celente told me he'd initiate the string of phone calls, and if he could get any input from the campaign, he'd talk to me in the morning.

The next morning, Friday, was filled with phone calls. All sorts of people had notions about how Ross Perot could best hang on to any votes he'd collected so far. Eventually, I narrowed it down to three possible avenues. The first, championed by a prominent strategist best known for his work for Democratic candidates, suggested we work on concepts that would defend Perot from a Clinton attack. Perhaps this person thought he had some inside information, but it didn't make any sense to me. Clinton had nothing to gain by attacking Perot, or by disturbing the delicate dynamics of the race in any way. Perot was in a position to hand the election to Clinton, and he hated George Bush. So we rejected that notion.

The second strategy argued for doing a thirty-second spot showing people reaffirming that they were voting for Perot, a mix of average American citizens and celebrity supporters like Willie Nelson, Cher, and Mohammed Ali. It's what I call a "bandwagon" commercial, a format that is best used to get people to jump *on* the bandwagon, not prevent them from jumping *off*. As a strategy, it would do nothing to overcome whatever obstacle was standing in the way of people finally pulling the lever for Perot. Also, celebrities in commercials often overwhelm the message they are supposed to deliver.

The third strategy was the only one I thought made sense, and it entailed tackling the wasted-vote argument head-on—convincing people that a vote for Perot was somehow not a waste, even though it was unlikely that he could win. I remembered a commercial we had conjured up for Wellstone's campaign that was never used. It was called "Ham Sandwich," and played off the old line of Sol Wachtler, chief judge of New York state, as he was being hauled off to prison: "You can get a grand jury to indict a ham sandwich, but that doesn't mean you're going to get a conviction."

Obviously we needed someone other than Perot to deliver the message. One of the directors I contacted was the first to suggest Ralph Nader. Whether Nader would do it, especially at the last minute, I had no idea. But he was the right person.

The commercial would open with Ralph sitting at a desk. Type would come up identifying him as "Ralph Nader, Consumer Advocate." What he would say was this:

> I'm Ralph Nader. Usually when people see me, I'm talking about something that doesn't work the way it's supposed to. But this time I'm going to tell you about something that *does* work—your vote.
>
> Throughout this election, politicians and the media have been saying that Ross Perot doesn't stand a chance on November 3rd. That if you're going to vote for Perot, you're throwing your vote away. Well, if this election is only about leaving the two parties in control and keep-

ing politics the way it's always been, then it's true—
George Bush and Bill Clinton might as well be running
against a ham sandwich as Ross Perot.

But I don't believe that's the case.

And even if it were, I'd vote for the ham sandwich.

Over the course of the weekend we developed seven TV
commercial concepts and two radio ideas that I thought mer-
ited being sent down the long and writhing road to potential approval. My favorite was a single uninterrupted take as
a camera pans down a wall of framed pictures of past presidents. First we see a statesmanlike Lyndon Johnson. Then a
devious-looking Richard Nixon. Then a troubled Gerald Ford,
with the picture askew and hanging precipitously from a single nail. Next we see a toothsome Jimmy Carter, then a grin-
ning Ronald Reagan, then a duplicate photo and frame of
Smilin' Ronnie. Finally a small picture of a concerned George
Bush, which falls to the floor, leaving an empty nail. And then
a blank wall.

The copy went like this:

In 1964, Lyndon Johnson promised you a Great Society.
It never happened.

In 1968, Richard Nixon promised you a secret plan to
end the war. It never happened.

(SILENCE AS THE CAMERA PASSES BY FORD, PAUSES
BRIEFLY, THEN MOVES ON WITHOUT COMMENT)

In 1976, Jimmy Carter promised you a better America. It
never happened.

In 1980, Ronald Reagan promised you'd be better off.

In 1984, Ronald Reagan promised you'd be better off.

People for Perot 1992

In 1988, George Bush promised you no new taxes. (PIC-
TURE FALLS OFF WALL, SOUNDS OF BREAKING GLASS)

(CAMERA MOVES TO BLANK WALL)

And they say it's a waste to vote for Ross Perot?

(SUPER "PEOPLE FOR PEROT" LOGO)

Don't waste your vote on politics-as-usual. Vote Independent Ross Perot for president.

By Sunday night I had scripts and storyboards ready to
send away the following morning. But that was the night
that Ross Perot was on *60 Minutes*. It was a devastating performance. Perot came across like a raving maniac. His explanation of why he quit the race earlier in the summer was a
disaster. And the next morning, little more than a week before
the election, papers were filled with stories about Ross Perot
obsessing about Black Panther assassination squads crawling
across his lawn.

Were the assassination squad stories a death wish by Perot?
Was he tanking the election because he was afraid he possibly
might win? Was he convinced he wouldn't win, so he was just
saying anything he felt like saying? Or had he just gone pure
Texas loco crazy?

Suddenly I was faced with a big decision. Should we really
help this guy? What if we somehow help him win?

Ultimately I decided to send the work. We weren't getting
paid for it—it was all done on spec—but I owed it to the people
who had worked with me on it to give it an audience. Plus, I
was pretty certain that Perot couldn't possibly win now.

But I didn't send the work, at least not right away. On
Monday night, I saw a Perot campaign commercial showing
Ross Perot behind a desk, making the case directly to voters
why a vote for him was not a wasted vote. It looked like it had

been produced that day, and Perot had none of his usual charm in the spot. He seemed tired and defeated—not a great look if you're trying to inspire the troops.

I reassessed my decision. If they had cut this spot in the aftermath of all the bad late publicity, they either figured having Perot speak directly to the issue was the most effective way to execute the strategy, or—given Perot's legendary frugality and the experience he'd had with ad people so far—they'd decided to throw in the towel on doing any other, more expensive commercials. Lack of money, though, didn't seem to be the reason. Perot had already spent $24 million on ad time in just the first two weeks of October. I dragged my feet until Tuesday, then finally faxed the ideas out.

All the air seemed to have gone out of the balloon. Wednesday night, six days after we first heard from the campaign, I was still waiting to hear something, anything, back from the campaign. By Thursday, I concluded they had given up and were not going to throw good money after bad. Or maybe the ideas just got lost on that long, twisted road from New York to Nashville to Dallas.

In the final analysis, we should all be properly amazed and impressed that Perot fared as well as he did. If the people left voting for him in the end were just the last of the true believers—and he still received nearly 20 percent of the vote—imagine how well he might have done if his advertising had been more effective, or had he avoided the many major missteps of his campaign, especially in the final days.

The question that nagged anyone who seriously considered the prospect of President Ross Perot was, could he govern? He had always put the day-to-day management of his companies in the hands of others, and he did not suffer bureaucracies gladly. Indeed, while he had gone out of his way to criticize government and many of the businesses he helped to direct, he always tended to shrug off the mantle of direct responsibility—during his service in the Navy, at IBM, after forming Electronic Data Systems (EDS), and during his stint on the General Motors board of directors.

Where more narcissistically impaired men would have a blind spot, I think Perot clearly recognized this foible in himself. Whether you attribute it to false modesty or believe he is being sincere, Ross Perot once said that although he has dreamed of being a beautiful pearl in an oyster, he sees himself more as a grain of sand . . . the grain of sand that irritates the oyster and thus produces the pearl.

Tale of the Tape

1992 Presidential Election

Bill Clinton (D)	43%	(44,909,806 votes)
George Bush (R)	37.5%	(39,104,550 votes)
Ross Perot (Ind.)	19%	(19,742,240 votes)

Wellstone 1996

Paul Wellstone won his Senate reelection race in 1996. But he lost something along the way—his independence from the mercenary, predatory clutches of Election Industry, Inc.

The Paul Wellstone of 1990 had changed a lot of people's apathetic views of politics, and had changed their lives in the process. His victory was truly revolutionary—the triumph of a different kind of candidate who ran a different kind of campaign—and his voters expected him to be a consistent voice for justice and reform. Those of us who knew the perils of Election Industry, Inc. had all the confidence in the world that if anyone could go to Washington and withstand the siren songs of money and power, it would be Paul Wellstone.

We were mistaken. Wellstone's 1996 reelection was less a victory for Paul and his politics than it was a victory for Election Industry, Inc. After five years in Washington, he had adopted a lot of the same mentality that pervades and perverts the partisan power struggle that Election Industry, Inc. uses to its advantage. These pollsters, pundits, and other treasure hunters took the biggest threat for electoral reform extant within their two-party duopoly and made him one of them. In 1990, ideas and imagination were more important than money, but by 1996 the Politics of Euphoria and Empowerment had transformed into Politics As Usual.

What voters saw in 1996 was not that the man they had elected in 1990 had misrepresented himself. What they saw was that even a good man could be corrupted by this lousy system. And in 1996, Paul was getting squeezed by the system from both sides.

The 1994 elections had been damaging to the psyche of Minnesota politics. Nationally, the midterms were a disaster for the Democrats; Newt Gingrich was now the Speaker of the House, and the Republicans had put out their Contract on America (as we called it). Closer to home, Minnesota's 1994 Senate race had been the most negative race—on both sides—the state had ever seen. Both candidates, former state legislator Ann Wynia and suburban Republican congressman Rod Grams, had been handled by Washington members of Election Industry, Inc. All the positivism and optimism and hopefulness surrounding Wellstone's victory, the excitement surrounding Ross Perot's 1992 Independent presidential campaign (in which he received 24 percent of Minnesota's vote), and the freshness that the boyish Arkansas governor Bill Clinton promised to bring into the White House—everything seemed dirty and tarnished after the Grams/Wynia slimefest.

Wellstone was not immune to the fallout, either. The 1994 Republican takeover had spooked a lot of incumbent Democrats, and Wellstone was hearing horror stories from the brain wizards within the Beltway, portents of doom from Democratic Party poobahs, and calcified conventional wisdom from

Election Industry, Inc. consultants. They told him how hard this election was going to be, how he would be unmercifully attacked, and how absolutely, definitively important it was that he win reelection—whatever the means to that end. Their admonitions undermined Paul's self-confidence and made him question the bond he had established with the people of Minnesota. Ultimately, Paul was turned. He had to win this election—at any cost.

There was some truth to what he was being told about the race ahead. Paul was going to be marked as the number one target for defeat by the Republicans. He was regularly ranked as the most liberal member of the Senate, so it was apparent that they would use that against him, and attack early and often.

Still, there were many reasons to be optimistic. As our own Mr.-Smith-Goes-to-Washington, Paul provided an unmistakable contrast to the mean-spirited, Gingrich-led Republican so-called Revolution. While it was obvious that the Republicans were not interested in the lesser members of society, Paul was seen as a person of integrity, one of the very few members of the Senate who would stand up for what's right even if everyone else was moving in a different direction.

Also, a year out, it was already shaping up to be a rematch. Rudy Boschwitz's candidacy had not been challenged within Minnesota's Republican Party; and while it is hard to deny anyone the shot at a rematch when the previous election was so close, I wondered about his motivation. It looked like a grudge match, like Boschwitz was thirsty for revenge, and I knew that wouldn't play well with those voters who were already beginning to have second thoughts about the 1994 Republican takeover and doubts about the Contract for America. The Perot vote in 1992 clearly showed that there was a whole new group of voters in Minnesota, political independents who wanted more and different choices. This key swing vote would not be very pleased or satisfied with a retread candidate, especially one who had already served twelve years in the Senate.

We had done our usual extensive targeting analysis, and divided Paul's target audiences into his Democratic base vote (which we had to have to win), the mostly independent swing vote (which we would need a majority of to win), and what we called the "opportunity" audience. These were voters who would not normally be in Paul's camp, but whom I saw an opportunity to convince. They included war veterans, senior men, small business owners and workers, laid-off big business executives and workers, doctors and health care professionals, hunters and fishers, and even possibly cops. Whatever we could pick up in these voter segments would give us a cushion if we failed to pick up enough of the swing vote, or—as I thought more likely—would contribute to a larger margin of victory.

Frankly, I didn't see any way the Republicans could beat us. Democrats were going to vote for Paul. So what the election would come down to was the swing vote. To me, it was obvious that Paul's swing vote in the 1996 election would be the Perot voters from 1992. Many of these voters, I was certain, had already considered and rejected Boschwitz once before, six years previous. And Paul had done a good job in his first term of standing up to monied special interests. As long as we could continue to portray him as an outsider fighting on the inside, we were pretty much unbeatable. The only way we could be beaten was if we beat ourselves.

Then I saw how real a possibility beating ourselves could be. I had been informed that hardly any of the key Minnesota people from Wellstone's 1990 election were going to be involved in his reelection campaign. But I wasn't prepared for how Washington-centric this campaign was going to be. Paul's Washington staff naturally had a vested interest in seeing him reelected; their involvement was fine with me, and they could be helpful in terms of research and coordination with legislative strategy and policy issues. But the campaign's key influencers in Washington turned out to be mostly professional political staff who had spent their lives working on Capitol Hill or in and around D.C. They were not authorities on what people in Minnesota were thinking—they were, literally, far from it. Having been marinated in the conventional wisdom of politics within the echo chamber of the Beltway, they would likely have an opinion on how we wanted to run the race, and their opinion would likely be wrong. With the laying on of the hands of the handlers of Election Industry, Inc., I feared even Paul Wellstone could be converted into just another politician—which was exactly what the people of Minnesota didn't want to see.

Almost a year before Election Day, the Beltway Bandits started circling the campaign. We agreed on nothing, and the biggest disagreements between Paul's other advisors and myself were about money. They were talking about spending $6 million, which I knew was a hell of a lot of money in Minnesota; we had gotten Paul elected on nearly $5 million less than that in 1990. But from the Election Industry, Inc. viewpoint, $6 million isn't very much at all. While that might be true in a campaign that was going to spend like drunken sailors in the final weeks of an election, my opinion has always been that much of that spending is a complete waste of money and, beyond that, annoying to voters, especially coming from a unique candidate like Paul.

The first disagreements about spending our money centered on our response to how we anticipated our opponents would spend their money—namely, attacking Paul. When the Republicans say you are their number one target, that means only one thing: that they intend to attack you early and often. In fact, the more I thought about how I would do this if I were Boschwitz, the more I believed that the Republican Party or the National Republican Senatorial Committee

(RNSC) would do the dirty work of attacking Paul Wellstone, allowing the Boschwitz campaign to stay out of the fray and save its money until the fall. It looked like we would be fighting on two fronts against two different but allied enemies, with only our own resources.

One of the most effective ways to combat attack ads, I believe, is to get out in front of them and ridicule them before they even start. Most attack ads are filled with such overstatements and such overheated rhetoric that the majority of viewers find them, literally, unbelievable. Upon repeated viewings—and attack ads are the ads Election Industry, Inc. tends to run at truly obscene media levels—voters just hate them. If we could cultivate this skepticism in advance of the attacks, we would neutralize much of their effect, "inoculating" Paul against their poison. That's why I wanted to do an early media buy. When the campaign asked what I would run, I showed them an ad I had developed called "Under Attack."

The ad took my strategy of ridiculing political attack ads over the top. I had found a lot of old cheesy monster and horror film footage, and by using a "blue screen" technique, we could shoot Paul talking to the camera, then insert the footage behind him. The end effect made him look like he was being attacked by huge scorpions, flying saucers with ray guns, and even Ming the Merciless, that dastardly evildoer from the old *Flash Gordon* TV series.

It's the same technique your local weatherman uses to superimpose the weather maps behind him on the nightly news. Paul would be addressing the viewer, oblivious to the potential mayhem taking place behind him. And in the final sequence, after Ming the Merciless appears on screen, we snuck in a photo of Rudy Boschwitz and even a shot of Newt Gingrich, superimposed as the great and all-knowing Oz.

We had wanted to get this spot ready by early spring, so we could launch it as soon as the Republicans fired their first volley, and keep it running sporadically throughout the spring to negate each new attack. My strategy was Rapid Preemption rather than Rapid Response. But the blockheads from Election Industry, Inc. nixed that idea; it wasn't until July, when the attacks were already flying, that we actually got to shoot the ad. The opportunity for inoculation had disappeared, and while I felt the ad would still be effective as a defense ad, the campaign thought Paul didn't look "senatorial enough." It was a rerun of the controversy over "Fast Paced Paul" in 1990, with a different cast. But this time the different cast won out.

The Republican attack ads started in earnest in early May. Most were ridiculously simple-minded—and predictable. Boschwitz's campaign apparently had studied the book *Professor Wellstone Goes to Washington,* written by two *Minneapolis Star-Tribune* reporters after the 1990 election, to figure out what they did wrong and what they needed to do better. I often joked during the 1996 campaign that I could always figure out what the Republicans or Boschwitz would do next by reading a few pages ahead of where they were in the book.

While the Republican National Committee and the NRSC were attacking Wellstone over the airwaves, the Boschwitz campaign was sitting tight—for the most part. What the Boschwitz campaign did do was put up a billboard nearby Wellstone's headquarters, depicting a cartoon that was supposedly Wellstone flying in a Mighty Mouse type of pose, with a big "W" on his superhero costume. Alas, the "W" was not for "Wellstone," but for welfare—Paul Wellstone was Welfare Man! (Previously the billboard called him "Paul Welfare.") Apparently Boschwitz's Election Industry, Inc. consultants thought they needed to use humor and that this was hilarious. Unfortunately for them, nobody else did.

The NRS attack ads were particularly simplistic: all one-note name-calling nonsense that eventually annoyed the hell out of every TV watcher in the state. They trumpeted the word "liberal" and applied it to Paul Wellstone every way they could think of—"embarrasingly" liberal, "ultra" liberal, "foolishly" liberal, "unbelievably" liberal, "liberally" liberal (OK, I'm kidding about that one)—as if this was news to the voters of Minnesota! It was just another example of Election Industry, Inc. fighting the last war. Because these tactics worked in 1994, they were certain they would work again in 1996, as if everything had been frozen in time for two years.

Even though the attack ads were risibly inept, Wellstone started to get more and more anxious about their effect. I tried to reassure him that our key swing voters were independent-minded enough to dismiss the attacks, and that the huge majority of them would not even start paying attention to the race until sometime in October. But as the relentless attacks went on, he became more and more agitated.

I had tried, with the "Under Attack" commercial, to get out ahead of the NRSC's attack ads and to ridicule them, but since the campaign's resistance had cost us that opportunity, I didn't want to make things worse by trapping Paul into fighting a second enemy this early in the campaign. It was evident to me that the Republicans were "playing" Paul—they wanted to goad him into spending down his war chest, to soften him up before the Boschwitz money started to be spent in earnest later in the year. It was a calculated provocation on their part.

And it was working. The campaign had been fixated on rapid response since the first stages of its formation. They were partially persuaded by my argument that this was a trap, and that it was too early to spend our "hard" campaign dollars versus the "soft" independent expenditure dollars the Republicans were using. So the campaign decided to respond not with ads, but through press releases.

That's a mistake: thinking you can answer attack ads by pointing out their lies and errors only through press releases and earned media. You can't. The paid media attacks go on and on, while the reporting on them is usually at best a one-day story—here today, forgotten tomorrow.

With the free media response strategy proving ineffective, as I knew it would, Paul demanded that we get on the air with some kind of rebuttal ad. I had long felt that the best thing we could do in our first TV spot to position Paul for reelection would be a reprise of "Fast Paced Paul," the spot that originally created his persona as a unique political figure in 1990. Fortunately, Paul had just cast major votes on student loans and campaign finance reform and the minimum wage.

"Faster Paced Paul" went on the air in early June, and it did its job. People were glad to have the same old Paul back, and even happier to hear that he had gotten something accomplished in Washington.

We also made news, and waves, when we turned a CNN report denouncing one of the Republicans' particularly heinous and inaccurate attack ads into a two-minute response ad sponsored by the state Democratic Party. Presenting the damning CNN piece in its entirety, the ad infuriated the state and national Republican parties, who threatened to sue. Their arguments about fair use of copyrighted material held no water, in my opinion, but the state Democratic Party backed down from what could have evolved into a landmark case and stopped running the ad.

Election Industry, Inc. has its own unique ways of measuring the success of ads (especially those that it doesn't create). This became painfully evident when the Wellstone campaign brought in two focus group moderators from the West Coast touting the latest technology in political polling, something called real-time dial testing. The technique calls for each person in the focus group to be given a handheld dial, then force fed about twenty different commercials in succession, most of them prepared for Wellstone, and some which had aired for Boschwitz. The participants were told to turn the dial in one direction if they saw or heard something they agreed with, and in the opposite direction if they saw or heard something they disagreed with. The dial was incremental: if they felt strongly one way or another, they should turn the dial far in that direction; if they only mildly agreed or disagreed, they should move it just a little from center.

This kind of technology is fraught with problems. The focus group was trying to replicate the viewer's everyday TV-watching experience, and participants were told to make believe they were sitting at home. But reality is overpowering. Who watches TV with twenty-four other people of your same age and sex, sitting in rigid rows of metal folding chairs, silently turning a dial to express your feelings? It was a completely artificial environment, and no leap of imagination or "visualization" exercise was going to change that.

Meanwhile, behind a one-way mirror in an adjacent room sat members of Wellstone's reelection campaign, including myself. As the commercials played in front of the focus group, they simultaneously appeared on a TV screen in the observation room. Each dial had been outfitted with a transmitter, so the respondents' actions could be aggregated instantly, and a computer would overlay a line graph over the commercial as it ran, indicating in real time the parts people liked or agreed with and the moments they disliked in each commercial.

Grown adults were beside themselves in the observation room. The general strategist at one point leaped to his feet and pointed to the TV screen, jabbing his finger in the air and shouting, "That's it! That's it! See how that spiked?! They love those words! We have to put those same words in all of our ads!" I sat in a corner of the room, trying to watch the audiences' faces. In over twenty years of making commercials and other audio and video communications, I have learned that the most honest reaction you can get is to watch a person's face the first time they see something. Most of the faces I was watching were drawn and frowning—far more engaged in the task at hand than what was playing on the screen.

The pollster and the strategist were ecstatic. The campaign manager was getting caught up in their enthusiasm. I was stupefied.

"You all gotta be kidding," I said. "All that was was a waste of people's time and our money and some perfectly good sandwiches."

They got argumentative, then angry, as I pointed out all of the problems with the research method.

"Ok, Mr. Smart Guy, how would you do it?" they demanded.

"Well, I wouldn't," I said. "But if I had to do something with these groups and if I was trying to get anything close to a real-world test, here's how I'd go about it. I'd have no moderators in there at all. I wouldn't introduce the people and I wouldn't have any chairs. I'd herd 'em into the room and let them have at the sandwiches and the soft drinks and the cookies. Meanwhile, I'd stick the TV in a corner of the room and run a loop of the commercials. When a commercial comes on that makes them stop talking to other people or makes them stop eating to watch, well, that's the commercial I would run. *That's* a real-world test."

The room suddenly got real quiet. But a lot of money had been spent on this testing. So needless to say, I was alone in my opinion.

Fortunately for us, the Election Industry, Inc. brain trust behind Boschwitz was no better. They were too invested in their relentless "embarrassingly liberal" attack ads to look for something different and more effective. If they had, they could have easily found Paul's Achilles heel in this election. To destroy Paul Wellstone, they needed to undo the image that most Minnesotans had of him as an elected official of integrity, conscience, and honesty. If they could accomplish that, everything else would crumble.

The evidence was there. Though Paul's work in the Senate had for the most part stayed admirably true to his stated ideals, he had waffled, flip-flopped, or taken opportunistic election year votes on a number of issues. He abandoned gays and lesbians in his vote in favor of the Defense of Marriage Act, which denied legal standing and domestic partner benefits to thousands of homosexuals. He was guilty of flip-flopping on allowing motorized vehicles into Minnesota's Boundary Waters wilderness area, saying one thing to environmentalists and city dwellers and something else to the residents and the businesses dependent on the tourism trade up north. He waffled on whether he would vote for an amendment banning flag burning.

And then there was campaign finance reform, an issue on which he came into the Senate sounding like a true firebrand. Since shortly after his inauguration, however, he had proven to be more like his new Senate colleagues than not. During his first run for the Senate, Paul promised to take out biannual ads listing all of his campaign contributions and expenditures. That never happened. He said he would not accept PAC money nor would he accept contributions of over $100 per year from any individual. Then he modified that position, and said he wouldn't take any out-of-state PAC contributions. Then he changed his mind again, and said he would take money from out-of-state PACs if they had some sort of affiliation to groups in Minnesota or ties to the state (nearly any organization can satisfy that condition). But after his first election, he suddenly began taking money from any PAC, anywhere. (He claimed he needed to retire his campaign debt, a number that kept increasing as he kept reclassifying old ex-

penses as campaign debt or adding new ones.) After finally re-
tiring his 1990 campaign debt two years later, he reverted back
to the original pledge, which held only until 1994.

Stating that he could not unilaterally disarm, and with his
1996 reelection campaign two years away, Wellstone again
began taking PAC contributions from any organization that
had a member in Minnesota—a pretty loose criterion. And in
December 1995, he dropped the individual contribution limit
of $100, criticizing the "rotten system" he was in, but not
walking the walk. Between 1990 and 1996, it was probably
easier to figure out the federal tax code than it was to figure out
who could give how much and when to Wellstone's campaigns.

These flip-flops and this doubletalking were the keys to
victory for the Republicans, not looking at our 1990 playbook
to see what we did right and they did wrong. And not their
one-note harping on the word "liberal." If the Republicans
could make people question Paul's integrity and honesty, if
they could demonstrate that the voters thought they elected
somebody different in 1990, but here he was six years later
walking and talking and quacking just like every other politician, the Republicans could have beaten Paul, even with a retread candidate like Boschwitz.

To distract from all the waffling, we kept emphasizing
throughout the campaign the one truly courageous vote Paul
did make in advance of his reelection: He was the only Senator
up for reelection to vote against the welfare reform bill. The
bill passed by a large margin, which made his vote all the more
remarkable. It would have been easy for Paul to rationalize
that it wasn't worth falling on a sword on this one issue and
handing ammunition to his opponent for an attack ad when
his side was going to lose regardless of his vote. Most politicians would take the path of least resistance and live to fight
another day for what they truly believe in. But on this issue,

Paul stood fast, while nearly every other Democrat—especially those facing reelection—cut and ran.

My biggest fear was that our campaign would somehow reveal how much like every other politician Wellstone had become. This culminated in a final showdown between me and the Election Industry, Inc. forces running the campaign. Paul had wanted us to do ads that depicted him talking about the issues to small groups of people. I was against it for a variety of reasons, first and foremost that it would look like every other political commercial for every other Washington politician. I was convinced that if we went this route, the Boschwitz campaign would need only to point to our commercials as evidence Paul Wellstone had "gone Washington."

Ultimately, I lost the battle—and the war. By the end of August, Election Industry, Inc.'s own Mandy Grunwald, a friend of both the Washington, D.C. pollster and the general strategist, was brought in to produce the campaign's ads. Mandy was more than happy to show Paul speaking to small groups of people; meanwhile our duties were reduced to buying and placing media, and producing only an occasional ad. Oddly, we were told we were being replaced for our inability to produce rapid response ads—even though we had figured out an ad and a strategy to neutralize the attacks in advance (which the campaign rejected); we had produced two effective defense ads, one for the campaign and one for the party (the campaign liked neither), and it was our rapid response commercial—written, produced, and aired all in one afternoon—that was instrumental in Paul's down-to-the-wire victory in 1990.

Moreover, the ads we did get on the air during the fall invariably performed better with audiences than Grunwald's ads on the same subject—at least according to standard methods by which Election Industry, Inc. measured audience response. In September and October, we were running tracking polls to help us keep tabs on the volatility of the electorate and to help us monitor the advertising's effectiveness. Occasionally, we would run ads produced by us and ads produced by Grunwald on the same message in the same week. We would regularly find that the Grunwald ad would need to run far more frequently than ours to reach the same level of audience comprehension. And many of our ads were only half as long—thirty seconds as opposed to the sixty-second ads Grunwald would produce, or fifteen-second ads as opposed to thirty seconds.

In the end, Wellstone won by nine points, 50 to 41. But at what price was his victory? The poor man's politician, Paul Wellstone, who made such an issue out of campaign finance reform and about how his opponent was going to repurchase his U.S. Senate seat in 1990, eventually outspent the Boschwitz campaign in 1996 by an amount that nearly equaled the total expenditures of his first campaign. In 1990, crass political dirty tricks by the Boschwitz campaign forced voters to hold their noses on the way to the polls. In 1996, cold political calculations by the Wellstone campaign caused his own supporters to hold their noses as they cast a joyless vote for the one politician they hoped would be different.

Tale of the Tape

Minnesota 1996 U.S. Senate General Election

Paul Wellstone (DFL)	50.3%	(1,098,493 votes)
Rudy Boschwitz (R)	41.3%	(901,282 votes)
Dean Barkley (Reform)	7%	(152,333 votes)

Getting Under
Your Opponent's Skin

As an incumbent, Republican Senator Rudy Boschwitz was used to people and the press taking shots at him, and he rarely lost his cool. In fact, he was something of a master of disguise. His silver hair, while not the true Senate–issue helmet-head of a Trent Lott or a Chris Dodd, was rarely out of place. The only time you'd see him sweat was when he wanted you to see him sweat, as he related in a fundraising memo to fellow Republicans: "Parades are great! Walk behind your car; don't ride. Rush over and shake some hands at the curb. Stop every 100 yards and conspicuously wipe the sweat off your brow."

Boschwitz would also wear light blue shirts rather than white, so voters could see the sweat stains under his arms and see he was "working hard." Unless, of course, he was tieless and wearing one of his trademark plaid shirts, a fashion statement calculated to make him look more like a regular guy and not the multimillionaire he was.

Most incumbents can afford to be pretty cool customers, because their defeat is so unlikely. But incumbents, like all candidates, are people; and people can do some unpredictable things.

Some campaigns set out intentionally to get under their opponent's skin. I never plan on doing this, but if it happens, I'm not going to complain.

Nobody, to my knowledge, has ever run a perfect campaign. And when you work for challengers—and especially underfunded challengers—this is something to hold on to, something to give you hope. All campaigns make mistakes. And the chances of a campaign making a really big gaffe are increased when the candidate is fixated on some burr under the saddle.

During Paul Wellstone's landmark upset victory over Boschwitz in 1990, I was surprised at how upset the senator got at one of our ads. It wasn't our best ad, and it didn't run very long. But Boschwitz became obsessed by it, to the point of distraction. He would bring it up long after it stopped airing.

The ad, which we called "Dust," had two purposes. It was intended to point out Boschwitz's antienvironmental voting record, and to highlight Wellstone's signature green school bus, which had proved to be a popular and recognizable symbol for the campaign. The ad had Wellstone standing beside one of the windows of the bus, where he would take his finger and draw little pictures in the dust on the window of the bus. The copy was written like a parable, or a children's story, and Wellstone was illustrating the story.

First he drew a smile, a nose, and eyeglasses (Boschwitz wore them, Wellstone did not). Then he drew a dollar sign in the dust. Next he drew a skull and crossbones. Then he drew a halo above the first illustration. At the end, he wiped away the face with the halo as the bus drove off.

The copy, delivered by one of my favorite voice actors, Harlan Saperstein, read:

Once there was a Senator named Rudy Boschwitz
Who took campaign contributions from polluters
Then worked behind the scenes to gut the Clean
    Air Act.
When it came time for reelection, he ran commercials
    that said he was an environmental champion.
But the people didn't believe him.
And they voted for somebody else.

Some ads have a target audience of one. For instance, if you want to talk directly to the CEO of a major corporation, you might buy a billboard outside the CEO's office. But this wasn't one of those situations.

We thought it was a good commercial in 1990, but not a great one. It was aimed at the voters, especially those voters who were concerned first and foremost about environmental issues. But it turned out to be most effective in affecting an audience of one: Rudy Boschwitz.

What was it about this environmental spot that drove him up a tree? He wasn't mad at the fundraising charges we made against him—in fact, he took great pride in his prowess as a fundraiser. (In the aforementioned memo to his fellow Republicans, he even boasted about it: "Nobody in politics—except me!—likes to raise money.") The caricature of him didn't bother him, nor did the sarcastic halo. Not even the charge that he was responsible for gutting the Clean Air Act.

What drove him batshit was the skull and crossbones, which came on screen not while we were talking about him, but while we fingered corporate polluters. And he couldn't forget it. He was still talking about it late in October, telling Paul in the campaign's last debate that it was unconscionable and reprehensible to associate him with a symbol that meant poison.

In all honesty, practically no one but Boschwitz himself ever made that connection, or mentioned the skull and cross-bones, or even talked about the ad. I never heard any conversation about it from the voters. We thought it was good, simple visual communication. But we could never have imagined or predicted the effect it would have on our opponent.

Today, most campaigns have adopted the Election Industry, Inc. tactic of having a party operative or campaign volunteer armed with a camera follow around the opponent. These poor grunts, who rarely realize what they're in for, are told to tail the opponent at press conferences, at speeches, and at any other public appearances or semipublic events. Generally this is just to unnerve the opponent—to give them the sense that someone is watching them at every moment. (And another reason why good, normal people no longer want to run for office.) In the event the candidate says or does something stupid, the opposition has footage that it can use later in an attack ad.

In the 1996 Wellstone-Boschwitz rematch, the soft-money shoe was on the other foot. Wellstone, who had eschewed political action committee (PAC) money in his 1990 race, was taking all he could this time around, because he felt he could not "unilaterally disarm" while being designated the Republicans' Public Enemy Number One. So Paul, under the direction of his Election Industry, Inc. fundraiser, was blithely running all over the country to pick up checks here and attend fundraisers there. This rampant fundraising led to a sense of paranoia that played in Paul's head throughout his entire re-election campaign.

Whenever a candidate pulls me aside to speak to me in private, I know I am about to hear nothing good. Paul called me aside in the spring of 1996. He tried to downplay it, but I could see he was worried and rattled by what he had to say. He didn't know how to tell me this, and didn't want to, but thought it better that his campaign be prepared to handle this than to have it pop up on us unexpectedly.

On a trip to California late in 1995 or early in 1996, Paul said, he was caught by one of these political paparazzi as he left a fundraiser at an extremely wealthy couple's extravagant home. (This would have been anathema to the Paul Wellstone of 1990, who made a big point of the fact that he was running for office to "represent the little fellers, not the Rockefellers.")

Telling me about it, Paul vacillated in his description of what happened. Apparently he was getting into the back seat of a sedan when either he or someone who was with him noticed the spy taping his exit. The story tended to change a little each time he told it. The first time Paul told me the story, the person he was with was handing him his coat as he was getting into the back seat of the sedan. In other tellings, Paul already had the coat and was pulling it on just before he got into the back seat of the sedan.

But the result was the same in both versions. Because of the angle of the camera, or because his companion was handing him his coat, or because he was throwing on his coat before getting into the car—well, it might have looked like he and his handler had spotted the camera and were throwing a coat over his head so he wouldn't be recognized.

Great, I thought. With the professional assassins of Election Industry, Inc. that the Republicans had working for them, if they do in fact have this footage, we will be treated to shots of Paul Wellstone converted to black and white, run in distorted slow motion, and looking like someone trying to dodge the cameras of *Hard Copy* or *60 Minutes*. Or he would simply resemble some prisoner trying not to be recognized on a perp walk into the courthouse. (Talk about not looking senatorial!)

Paul maintained (more to reassure himself, I think, than me) that he was inculpable, and that it was probably nothing, and that they probably didn't get a good shot anyway, but his eyes told a different story. He kept saying that what happened wasn't what it might look like, but it might look like that, and if it does, well, then what do we do?

I told Paul the only thing you can tell a candidate in that situation: don't worry about it. We'll handle it.

First of all, I said, given the number and intensity of the attacks he'd seen to date, don't you think they'd be running it by now if they had anything worth using? (Actually, I didn't believe this myself—they certainly could be saving it for late in the campaign, when more people would be paying attention. But I wanted Paul to stop obsessing over it.) Secondly, I said, for as many voters who watch those "gotcha!" shows there are as many who feel that the shows are "junk journalism" and not credible. So if the Republicans used something in this vein, it would likely be seen by many as overstepping the boundaries of clean, hard, campaigning. (Not that this was going to stop them.)

Right up until Election Day evening, I think Paul kept expecting to see that footage in a Boschwitz commercial. But we never did.

Which leads me to conclude they never had it in the first place. Maybe the kid was holding an empty camera.

Don't laugh. If your only purpose is to get under your opponent's skin, why waste all that money on tape or film?

Negative Campaigning and
Rapid Response

Early on in my first political campaign, Paul Wellstone's opponent aired a TV ad making claims about himself that the Wellstone camp told me were patently not true.

No problem, I said. We'll just present the evidence to the stations or to the election board or whomever, and the spots will have to come off the air.

One of the few more senior staffers on the campaign looked at me like I was a child, a child whose dewy eyes badly needed wiping. "The election board?" he snickered.

My sense of justice was being impugned at the same time I was being ridiculed. "Or the stations," I said, self-righteously.

"This is a federal race. Congress passed laws saying their ads can't be censored, and stations have to run them. That ad isn't coming down."

I was wide-eyed. "You mean you can *lie* in political advertising?" I asked in a way that must have seemed like the second coming of Pollyanna.

My political education had begun.

In advertising—commercial speech—there are all kinds of restraints and regulations about what you can and cannot say. In political free speech, there are none.

In the commercial field, someone is always looking over your shoulder to make sure you are telling the truth and can document any claims made in your advertising. Your competitors scour every word of every ad, looking to see if there is something they can challenge on legal grounds as false or misleading. The Federal Trade Commission (FTC) and Federal Communications Commission (FCC) have rules governing what can and can't be said. Special rules apply for special product categories, like alcoholic beverages or advertising to children. State attorneys general are ever vigilant for consumer fraud or false advertising cases (mostly because they generate so much positive publicity for the Attorney General as Consumer Watchdog—sort of a Mini-Me version of Ralph Nader.)

Politics has none of these. The closest thing politics has to a regulatory body is the inept and impotent Federal Election Commission (FEC), whose idea of harsh justice is to fine a campaign a few thousand dollars for gross fundraising abuses totaling in the millions. So the candidates and campaigns of Election Industry, Inc. regularly take advantage of the situation, running advertising—especially negative advertising—which takes the thinnest skin of truth and stretches it well beyond the breaking point.

The question the media always ask in analyzing negative ads is, who's right and who's wrong?

The question most voters are usually asking is, who cares?

• • •

"You're a big stupidhead!"

"No, *you're* a big stupidhead!"

Most voters like to think of themselves as adults. Which often leaves them scratching their heads when the candidates of Election Industry, Inc. unfailingly revert to the childish name-calling and "he-started-it-first" accusations that are rampant in our political campaigns.

Americans today admit they get most of their election information from campaign ads. That should be a frightening thought for all of us.

Because what passes today as political discourse is tearing at our social fabric. What masquerades as ideas in our campaigns are "gotcha!" type ads which employ associations and leaps of logic that are not only false, but intentionally misleading. As a consequence, we are now seeing our political culture finally pay for the seeds of discontent it has so licentiously cast about for so many years.

Only recently have political practitioners come out and admitted what I have been saying for over a dozen years now: negative campaign tactics and attack ads are less an aggression against opponents than they are an assault on our democracy.

In a survey of political professionals done in 2002, 37 percent said it was acceptable to use negative advertising to hold down voter turnout and to focus on the negative personal characteristics of an opponent rather than on issues.

Political consultants think that's smart.

I think it's despicable.

Any political practitioner who would deliberately and cynically attempt to prevent citizens from participating in an election and not exercise their most cherished constitutional right—the right to vote—is no friend of democracy.

And since most of our citizens are now getting the majority of their political information from political advertising, is it any wonder why, when negative advertising rears its ugly head, they choose not to vote, and show little interest in what goes on in Washington?

Discouraging Americans from voting and from scrutinizing their performance in office may help keep incumbents from the two major parties and their allies in Election Industry, Inc. in power. But it is not making our country any better.

So what, exactly, is negative campaigning?

To most voters, negative campaigning means negative advertising. And negative advertising means attack ads.

But negative campaigning is often not this public. For example, many Election Industry, Inc. campaigns use spurious direct mail attacks late in a campaign—attacks that tend to stay out of the public eye and usually take place so close to Election Day that the damaged opponent has little opportunity to respond. Other devious Election Industry, Inc. tricks include "push polling"—a telephone tactic where the callers use the guise of a survey questionnaire to spread false information about a campaign's opponents. (Push polling is just one more good reason not to cooperate with pollsters.)

Still, by far the most prevalent form of negative campaigning is the attack ad. The good news is that attack ads have become so expected and so discredited that they are rarely a good use of a campaign's money. (But then, spending money wisely has never been a strong suit for most political campaigns.) Many attack ads are immediately dismissed by the electorate, who see them for what they are: arguments without merit that attempt to attain credibility by shouting at the top of their lungs as loudly and as often as possible. In this case, the squeaky wheel should not get the grease: it's just a squeaky wheel, symptomatic of old wheezing machinery that needs a complete overhaul rather than a quick fix.

Voters have an innate sense of skepticism about negative

ads. They have learned through the years not to take what politicians say at face value, an attitude that often extends to a candidate's ads.

Politicians and the media like to debate what is negative and what is not, but most voters already know the difference. Voters are fairly discerning about the difference between attack ads—those *ad hominem,* slash-and-burn slices of overheated rhetoric, questionable accuracy, and distorted facts—and legitimate contrast advertising, which presents a fair-minded (though ultimately pejorative) comparison of policy differences or voting records among candidates.

Contrast advertising is not only educational for individual voters, but necessary to an informed electoral process. In an election with an incumbent, the challenger must make the case for change by drawing distinctions between himself or herself and the record of the incumbent. Otherwise, voters tend to default to the status quo. (In general, Americans are a fair-minded electorate: we do not throw somebody out of a job without a good reason.)

Attack ads can be a big gamble because of the risk of backlash. Voters make up their own minds about a candidate's character, based upon what they see with their own eyes and feel in their own hearts. A candidate or campaign who attempts to do this work for the voters can expect to pay the consequences, succinctly stated by that noted political philosopher Pee-Wee Herman, who observed, "I'm rubber, you're glue; what you say bounces off me and sticks to you."

What's more, voters are attracted to strong, confident leaders with an aura of optimism about them. Negative ads—besides being the antithesis of positivism—tend to tarnish campaigns, and the petty bickering we regularly witness in our campaigns demeans every candidate who takes part in it.

The real risk for any campaign going negative is if the

responsibility for the negativity becomes associated only with one side. This is why so many attack ads are developed by so-called independent groups, funded entirely by soft money contributions. It's also why the truly nefarious campaign tactics are usually practiced out of the public eye. If attack ads backed by massive media buys are the "carpet bombing" of the campaign wars, "stealth bombing" an opponent via push polls and negative mailings aimed at a specific portion of the electorate are now the preferred stratagem.

Negativity in an election becomes particularly problematical for the two major political parties when there is a viable independent or third-party candidate in the race. If the negativity in the race becomes associated with both major-party candidates—a typical situation in most elections, since the knee-jerk reaction of Election Industry, Inc. is "when attacked, attack back"—the voters may say "a pox on both your houses" and either stay home or vote for the third-party candidate.

But by far the most insidious practice involving negative advertising is the conscious use of negative tactics to hold down voter turnout among certain groups. This cowardly act, most commonly practiced by the side that has the most to gain when fewer voters show up at the polls, works against the very notion of participative democracy and diminishes the voice of the people.

The conventional wisdom among pollsters and consultants these days is that a winning campaign must first slice-and-dice the electorate, then use wedge issues to incite likely voter groups and subdivide the vote even further. It's one of the reasons why in any given election, half or more of eligible voters will not show up. It's also a reason why candidates speak in pandering blandishment rather than strong positions or ideas whenever they're before an audience not made up of single-issue voters.

Negative Campaigning and Rapid Response

Too much of modern politics is *divide et impera* rather than *e pluribus unum*.

If we can't get politicians and the major political parties and Election Industry, Inc. to knock off the incessant negativism of their campaigns, how can higher-minded candidates defend themselves when attacked?

The conventional wisdom of Election Industry, Inc. holds that when attacked, you must respond at once (and unfortunately, that response usually takes the form of a counterattack). After all, "a lie unchallenged becomes the truth."

This strategy of immediate rebuttal, known as "rapid response," has become a truism of doctrinaire campaign thinking. But there are a lot of flaws in this strategy.

First of all, for reasons discussed above, not all negative advertising is as effective as the campaign being attacked assumes it is. Candidates and their campaign workers tend to scrutinize the airwaves and see every attack ad as a personal affront or vendetta. But much of it is invisible to voters, who often dismiss it when they notice it, and these ads open the attacking party to voter backlash, to criticism from the press, and—more often than not—surrender the moral high ground to the candidate being attacked.

Secondly, responding to attacks can often validate those attacks in the minds of the voters as well as in the press. It also, in public relations parlance, "keeps the story alive." I have seen many a one-day news report turn into a weeks-long harangue because campaigns take the bait of a spurious negative attack and attack back. The press covers the original allegation, often decides that there must be some truth to it because the candidate being attacked seems so sensitive about it, then covers the counterattack and the response—or counter-counter-attack—of the original attacking candidate.

In the meantime, the voters lose interest.

Third, responding to attacks immediately takes you off your own message and puts your campaign on the defensive. Suddenly, you are playing on the other candidate's turf and letting them set the agenda for the campaign. I have seen millions of dollars wasted when a campaign loses its focus on what it must accomplish and is distracted instead by responding to charges from the other side. Eventually your campaign does not have enough money to accomplish its own goals, because you spent so much money defending itself against attacks that the voters may not have been paying any attention to anyway.

There are two good response or defense strategies against negative campaigning and attack ads. One is to inoculate your candidate against the attacks, especially when you know being attacked is inevitable. The other good defense is to ridicule the attacks, as we did for Paul Wellstone in 1996.

Often the attackers become their own undoing. Consider Al Gore. His campaign spent so much time attacking his opponents—first Bill Bradley, then George W. Bush, and finally even Ralph Nader—that they failed to give voters an authentic sense of who Al Gore was, and why they should vote for him. Gore's attacks did nothing to help his likeability, and actually enhanced George Bush's likeability.

With attackers like these, who needs to respond?

Let Them Stay Home

Less than 50 percent of eligible voters—American citizens over the age of eighteen—voted in the last presidential election. Less than 20 percent of eligible voters are voting in some major municipal elections. In many states and municipalities, especially depending on the election, turnout is even lower.

In fact, only about 50 percent of eligible voters take part in any given election. That's our high-water mark. Influenced by Election Industry, Inc., we now consider it a success and a triumph for democracy if only half of the eligible voters participate in an election.

How did we get this way?

Some people are conscientious about their vote and won't vote on an issue or for a person they know little or nothing about. For others, the sound of a name or the position on a ballot or party affiliation is reason enough to cast their vote.

Some experts blame ignorance, some apathy. Some people just don't know and really don't care.

In my experience, most people take their vote seriously. People in America know they live in a democracy, that their vote is an important and cherished right, and that it is the very essence of being an American. They want to vote. They intend to vote. And then, something happens.

That something is no accident.

There are good reasons for not voting. Some people are extremely busy, or out of town, or are homebound—they physically can't leave the house. Before you judge these people, first try voting absentee yourself. The hoops and obstacles most states put in the way of citizens being able to freely exercise their franchise to vote is truly wrong-headed. Why are elections limited to certain hours of a single day? Why can't someone vote by mail, by phone, by proxy, or over the internet? We're in the twenty-first century now, you know.

We spend untold millions on our campaigns with so-called political professionals every election cycle. Yet we spend relatively little money on the election itself. And we leave the administering of our elections in the hands of (admittedly well-meaning) amateurs and volunteers. Our way of casting votes has not been significantly upgraded in the last half-century.

If Election Industry, Inc. wanted more people to vote, we would have more and easier ways of voting.

Another reason people don't vote is because we do a lousy job of follow-up on our campaigns. Many citizens dutifully go to the polls on Election Day, cast their vote, and then have absolutely no idea what happens as a result. In most parts of the country, the media have decided that people aren't interested in politics. So elections get some reporting just before they take place, and maybe a story or two of analysis immediately after, but that's it. By and large, the voters are out of the picture and ignored until we're begging them to show up again, two years later.

Political parties and elected officials do a bad job of tying a person's vote to meaningful change in his or her daily life, mostly because they don't want their campaign promises scrutinized and they don't want the responsibility of providing accountability to their voters. After all, they won't need that person's vote again for another two years or four years or six years. That's their excuse. But what's the media's excuse?

Most of the success my company has had in the political arena is because we take a consumer marketing paradigm and have found a way to make it effective in elections. One of the most basic marketing tenets is "get 'em young." People who establish a brand preference early in life tend to stay with that brand. For instance, chances are good that if you grew up eating Cheerios, you still eat them today.

But if getting 'em young is the key to the future of our democracy, the future isn't very bright. A recent survey commissioned by the National Association of Secretaries of State projected that only 32 percent of voters age eighteen to twenty-four voted in the 1996 presidential election, and only 20 percent in the 1998 elections. By comparison, in the 1972 election when I was first able to vote, 50 percent of young people participated.

Why so low? It's not because young people aren't committed to making the world a better place. In that survey 94 percent said "the most important thing I can do as a citizen is help others," and social cause volunteerism among young people is at record high levels.

But 58 percent of the respondents claimed "you can't trust

politicians because most are dishonest," and 64 percent said "government is run by a few big interests looking out for themselves, not for the benefit of all the people."

And 66 percent of these young people believed their generation has an important voice. Except—"no one seems to hear it."

It would seem that voting has an image problem.

Over the past couple of decades, no doubt you've seen all kinds of political party flacks and pundits and think-tank members and candidates and good government types and various other members of Election Industry, Inc. take to the airways to admonish or demand or beg you to vote.

Don't believe them. They're lying.

Politicians and pundits and party officials look at these voter turnout figures and tsk-tsk that low voter participation is bad for our democracy. The truth is, these are often the same people who secretly believe it is too high. They are certain these turnout figures contain far too many people who are ignorant of what or who they're voting for, who vote too whimsically and haphazardly, and who don't do their homework.

What they really mean is, go to the polls and vote if you're going to vote the way they want you to vote. Otherwise, they'd much prefer you just stay home.

With all the money focused on elections today, campaigns and political parties have more ways than ever to identify and target and persuade the people they want to vote, and to make you vote the way they want you to vote. As far as Election Industry, Inc. is concerned, participation in our democracy is only good as long as it is predictable.

Political parties don't want independent-minded voters going to the polls. They want like-minded voters going to the polls. They and their pollsters want to know what issue is most important to you, and where you stand on that issue. Then—

and only then—do they care or want to know if you intend to vote. If you're with 'em, golly gee yes, they want you to vote, and they'll spend plenty of money telling you how right you are to think the way you think and vote the way you do. They'll even arrange a ride to the polls for you.

If you're agin 'em, however, they will do everything they can to make you stay home, including making it difficult for you to get *into* the polls once you get to the polling place. Sometimes—as we saw in our last presidential election—they make it difficult for your vote to count *even after you've cast it.*

I don't know about you, but no matter how cynical I get, I still have an abiding faith in the basic principles of democracy and in the people's ability to decide among candidates. Voters generally are quite good about identifying a phony. Therefore, I believe that everyone even remotely involved in politics has a duty to be in favor of the highest possible voter participation.

That ought to be the one thing we all can agree on. A conscious attempt to depress voter turnout is the lowest of all political dirty tricks.

Conscious or not, that's the direction we are heading. Election Industry, Inc. feeds us a steady diet of increasingly negative and meaningless political ads. The numbing sameness of most political candidates, whose every move and position is defined by pollsters, and the dominance of extremists in both political parties have brought us to this serious erosion in voter participation. As the noise of political campaigns and the false fury of political candidates become more and more irrelevant to the lives of most of us, the only sensible response seems to be Mark Twain's: "I never vote. It only encourages them."

But voter turnout is the last effective check and balance we have against the untrammeled influence of big money and special interest groups in politics. It's a simple equation: the lower the voter turnout, the greater the influence of money in that election, and the better the opportunity for monied special interest groups to control the result of that election.

Political spinmeisters and the two big political parties benefit when independent-minded voters who are not captive to any party choose to stay home. Consultants and pollsters know the buttons to push to motivate party regulars—especially the extremists and one-issue voters—and they always show up. Political parties also have greater influence in low-turnout elections, because their get-out-the-vote efforts are aimed at the party faithful—again, people who are sure to show up—and at voters who are learning their way.

In short, when the undecided choose not to decide and stay home, it puts political parties, political consultants, and pollsters in control of the election.

Independent-minded voters are the voters who frighten these professionals and who act as the safety valve for the system. When independents show up to vote, they become the great unknown. They are dangerous. They have no fealty to the two major political parties or to Election Industry, Inc.

They are those who refuse to be controlled, and it is they who control each election.

DFL Gubernatorial Primary 1998

H ome to two recent vice presidents who later headed presidential tickets, Minnesota's political landscape had long been dominated by the Democratic Farmer Labor (DFL) Party. However, by 1998 the Democratic state of Humphrey and Mondale had been slipping in and out of the Republican column since the DFL glory days of the 1960s and '70s. There were even years in the late 1980s when the governor and both senators came from the Minnesota Independent Republican Party. (The "Independent" was added in the 1970s, to distance the state party from Richard Nixon and the Watergate scandal, only to be discarded again in the 1990s.) Yet the elders of the DFL arrogantly continued to act as if putting "DFL" behind your name automatically got you 40 percent of the vote.

Some of the party's problem was indicated by its multipart name. The once-dominant coalition of family farmers, miners from the Mesabi Iron Range, and other blue-collar workers still carried the party banner; but they were now outnumbered almost three to one by urban Democrats from the Twin Cities, whose priorities differed dramatically from the social and fiscal conservatism of their rural counterparts. By the 1990s, the DFL was controlled by an old-boy (and old-girl) network of leftists who kept nominating ultra-liberal candidates with little chance or ability to win. Increasingly, these candidates had to choose between saying one thing to city voters and another to the rest of Minnesota, which—particularly those farmers in the west and the south—was leaning more Republican as time went on.

The obvious potential for party infighting was made worse by a political calendar that left plenty of time for divisive public battles and little time for unity and recovery. The state nominating convention was held in June, but the primaries that actually determined the nomination did not take place until after Labor Day, often barely six to eight weeks before the general election. To make matters even more interesting, Minnesota's open-primary system allowed Republicans to choose to vote in the DFL primary, and vice versa, opportunities each party sometimes used to put into the general election an opponent they perceived as weaker.

The Democrats viewed 1998 as an opportunity. The popular moderate Republican governor, Arne Carlson, whose Democratic opponent in his 1994 reelection campaign, John Marty, had drawn the lowest statewide Democratic vote in memory, was stepping down. His handpicked successor, St. Paul mayor Norm Coleman, was perceived by many as being too slick and ambitious. Coleman was a former Democrat who had done wonders in his five years as mayor of the state's long-dormant capital city, but he had left the DFL only a few years earlier because the Republican Party offered more room for rapid ascension. To oppose this prodigal son, the DFL turned to some of the biggest names from the Minnesota Democrats' glory years—only to find a pale imitation of the greatness that the party once represented. In what the *New York Times* dubbed the "My Three Sons" race, the progeny of Hubert Humphrey, Walter Mondale, and former Minnesota governor and JFK cabinet member Orville Freeman all squared off for the Democratic nomination.

They weren't alone. A fourth big name in the race was Mark Dayton. The Dayton's department store name had been emblazoned on ads, shopping bags, delivery trucks, and most Minnesotans' consciousness since birth. As heir to the Dayton's and Target department store fortune, former state auditor Dayton had the deepest pockets of anyone in the race.

Leading the field was the current attorney general Hubert H. ("Skip") Humphrey III, who in June of 1998 won a land-mark settlement against the big tobacco companies, bringing billions of dollars into the state and making him the odds-on favorite. Humphrey had run for the U.S. Senate in 1988 and had shown himself to be nothing like the "Happy Warrior" candidate his father had been. But he had widespread support from the party (and, more importantly, its biggest donors), as well as the most magical name in Minnesota political his-tory.

There was one other candidate: our candidate, Doug John-son. Fondly known as "Dougie" around the State Capitol, Tax Committee chairman Johnson was the lone candidate from outside the metro area. He had already proven himself to be an institution among his constituents on the Iron Range, the state's northern mining region, to whom he had delivered un-told amounts of tax dollars. In the battle of surnames, though "Johnson" was less distinguished than his competitors, it was also the most common name in this heavily Scandinavian state.

Heading into the statewide convention, the rest of the pack had already fallen far behind Humphrey. Ted Mondale was clearly the least experienced of the bunch. With only eight years as a state senator, at forty-two, he was young and looked younger. Hennepin County Attorney Mike Freeman had the presumed support of the state's labor unions, but little charisma and popular support. Dayton had been badly defeated in a 1982 Senate bid, and had spent the ensuing years away from the political spotlight.

The 1998 DFL state convention was held in St. Cloud, a small city in the middle of the state, about ninety minutes from Minneapolis/St. Paul. Because the convention is historically controlled by party zealots—mostly far-left liberals whom time has passed by—the candidate with the party's endorsement of late rarely won either the primary or the general election. Still, both Humphrey and Freeman opted to put up a pitched and expensive battle for the June endorsement.

First on the agenda, as usual, was a day devoted to protocol and convention rules fights—characterized in 1998 by the passage of a resolution asking delegates, alternates, and spectators to refrain from wearing any fragrances in the convention hall because other delegates might have a sensitivity to them. Setting aside for the moment the notion that these leftist delegates aren't always completely up to snuff on their personal hygiene—which would argue for *more* deodorant, cologne, and perfume rather than less—many participants felt that the controversy only served to make the party look completely foolish. When Doug Johnson showed up the next day and found out about the resolution, he said, "this is the most ridiculous thing I've ever heard—I'm going fishing!" and promptly left for his lake cabin up north.

Both Humphrey and Freeman remained, and seemed committed to a duel to the death. The arm twisting of delegates went on late into the evening. Both sides spent lots of money on balloons and literature and signs and floor staff. After a long, drawn-out battle, Freeman finally prevailed, due in large part to his ability to organize the party faithful and his support from the unions. The effort had drained his coffers, however, so the Freeman campaign left St. Cloud victorious but underfinanced for the real battle: the September primary fight ahead.

We spoke with Freeman about working on his campaign, but decided against it; he selected Washington, D.C. consultant Joe Slade White. Humphrey went with his long-time political consultants, Squier Knapp from D.C., and Mondale chose the D.C. firm Cosgrove McWilliams Smith. All were entrenched members of Election Industry, Inc.

Dayton, with whom we also spoke, struck me as alternately too tightly wound and too loosely wrapped for a stressful campaign. He went through three or four campaign managers during the election, and the last campaign manager ended up being his driver.

Though he was far less known (and dramatically less funded) than the others, Johnson didn't have their baggage. Humphrey was often perceived as personally inept and bailed out by a crackerjack staff. He seemed unable to escape the long shadow cast by his father. Freeman lacked warmth and the common touch and had a phoniness about him. Mondale was considered an inexperienced lightweight, and Dayton was perceived by many to be too rich and a loose cannon.

Three-way elections are far different from one-on-one races, and five-way elections are even more complicated. Despite the advantages of all the other candidates in money, resources, and name recognition, and despite Humphrey's huge boost from the tobacco trial, if the primary vote could be fractured enough, an underfunded candidate like Doug Johnson might slip through.

Doug had another advantage: he was demonstrably the smartest candidate in the race. His many years at the Capitol and his mastery of state finances made him formidable in any debate. And he was beloved by his Iron Range constituents; you would be hard-pressed to find someone on "da Range" who didn't have a good word for "Dougie," or who hadn't benefited directly from something he had done for them.

Our campaign did not have anywhere near the money or the resources to both introduce Doug and attack front-runner Humphrey. Our strategy for Doug was simple: boost his name recognition, demonstrate that he is smart, play to the outstate vote, hope for crossovers, and pray that the vote gets fractured enough that Humphrey comes back to the field and Johnson could slip through in a five-way race. The others were going to have to attack Humphrey, not us—besides not having enough resources, we wanted Doug to be perceived as being as nice as Humphrey, but smarter and more competent.

In a five-candidate race, debates can be crucial. In this case, they were also quite plentiful, and very revealing about our opponents' strategies. Humphrey, it became immediately clear, was going to try to stay out of the fray as much as possible. This approach was also designed to mask his shortcomings as a debater. Easily flustered and overly reliant on his notes, Skip Humphrey was as long-winded as his famous father but not as skilled: he would go on as long as you'd let him, and never really say anything.

His filibuster strategy in the debates was indicative of his entire campaign strategy: avoid doing anything stupid or controversial, sit on his big lead, and run out the clock to September. These kinds of campaign strategies, which are all too common in Election Industry, Inc., have a tendency to diminish candidates—you can *survive* an election doing this, but you will never take command of the election.

If Skip's numbers were going to come down far enough for others to catch him, the candidates trailing him were going to have to attack him. Mondale wouldn't attack first—right or wrong, his campaign stubbornly refused to see anyone other than the Republican nominee as the opponent, and spent most of its time and energy attacking Norm Coleman. Freeman tried to attack Humphrey during debates, but at well over six feet tall and two hundred pounds, he looked like a middle linebacker going after your short, pudgy grandfather. With his campaign's financial problems well known—the party endorsement had little financial value in the primaries, and the party leadership's reluctance to help him led to the prevailing notion that the party was lying down and waiting for Humphrey—Freeman also looked desperate when resorting to these verbal attacks.

Dayton was the wild card. He wasn't going anywhere unless it was at the expense of Humphrey, and he was strange enough to do anything, party niceties be damned. But the candidates' positions were so close that there was little room for Dayton to wedge himself between Humphrey and Freeman, and his attempts to do so in debates got him nowhere.

Curiously, the one candidate who did draw a clear contrast between himself and all of the Democratic candidates wasn't a Democrat at all.

In a benighted attempt to lure the Republican-endorsed candidate, Norm Coleman, to participate in the DFL debates, the organizers usually opened them to all candidates of any party or persuasion. Coleman, of course, was not about to be trapped into debating and being attacked by five Democrats, and said he would wait to debate the Democratic nominee in the general election, thank you very much. But candidates from the Libertarian Party, the Green Party, and other minor parties often filled the stage alongside the Democrats. So did the Minnesota Reform Party candidate, former pro wrestler, bit actor, and talk radio host Jesse Ventura. Ventura took every opportunity to appear at every debate and contrast his politics to those of the Democratic candidates, directly in front of a (mostly) Democratic faithful. Aiming barbs at "career politicians" and roundly lumping them all together, Ventura scored a lot of points with the audiences at the debates, especially working-class Democrats.

The decision to open up the primary debates was one that would cost Democrats dearly. Third-party politics was alive and well in Minnesota, at least whenever a credible candidate could be found. By 1998, I knew full well that there were a lot of independent-minded voters in Minnesota. Although we didn't know it at the time, the swing voters who elected Paul Wellstone in 1990 were a precursor to the 24 percent Ross Perot would get in the state in 1992. His remarkable showing—nearly one out of every four Minnesota voters had voted Perot for president in 1992!—gained major-party status for the Reform Party in Minnesota. And Perotistas were clearly the swing voters in Paul's 1996 reelection victory. Mostly conservative, older white males, they didn't agree with Wellstone on any one single issue, but, in the words of one of these supporters: "I think he's honest and he votes for what he truly believes in, and there oughta be at least *one* of those sons-of-bitches in the United States Senate!"

As summer drew to a close and we began to prepare for the candidates' important appearances at the Minnesota State Fair, we decided our best bet to differentiate Doug Johnson was to run him as a Minnesota version of Huey Long. Doug, unlike the legendary Louisiana political character, was a dedicated and smart public servant. Like Huey Long, though, he had always delivered for his constituents, and brought millions of dollars of institutional and infrastructure improvements to rural Minnesota.

But Doug's fundraising never caught fire, and we were only able to afford a few very inexpensive TV commercials and some radio spots. Still, we found some reason to hope at the State Fair. Plenty of rank-and-file union members pledged to

Freeman by their leadership told us in no uncertain terms that once the polling curtain closed, they were going to do the right thing and stand by the man they affectionately called "Dougie."

In the end, they were true to their word, but it wasn't nearly enough. Though the polls showed Johnson with far less than 5 percent support only a few days before the primary, Doug finished in a remarkable second place tie with the endorsed candidate, Freeman, each of them garnering 19 percent of the vote. Doug carried six of the state's eighty-seven counties; but Humphrey carried the other eighty-one, the runaway winner with 37 percent of the primary vote, nearly as much as his next two competitors combined. Mark Dayton finished with 17 percent and Ted Mondale was far back with 8 percent.

Despite his last place finish, Mondale ran a good campaign and arguably accomplished the most, overcoming his lightweight image and positioning himself for future races. (In fact, as governor, Ventura would later appoint him to run the Metropolitan Council, perhaps the most visible government planning position in the metro area.) But it was Dayton who would next run again, in the 2000 U.S. Senate race, where he would defeat a very weak Republican incumbent in an election that would cost him an unheard-of (in Minnesota) $14 million. Instead of the weird commercials—including ads that showed him bungee jumping and deflecting pucks as a hockey goalie— that marked his 1998 gubernatorial run, in 2000, Senator-to-be Dayton utilized the time-honored strategy of Election Industry, Inc.: telling people what they wanted to hear, delivering different—and sometimes contradictory—messages to different audiences, and blowing away his underfunded opponents with millions upon millions of dollars of campaign ads.

Our own candidate in the 1998 primary, Doug Johnson, went down in Minnesota election history as little more than a footnote. But not in my estimation. Because if we hadn't worked for DFL gubernatorial candidate Doug Johnson, there never would have been a Governor Jesse Ventura.

Tale of the Tape

Minnesota 1998 DFL Primary

Hubert H. Humphrey III	37%	(182,562 votes)
Mike Freeman	19%	(93,714 votes)
Doug Johnson	19%	(91,888 votes)
Mark Dayton	17%	(88,070 votes)
Ted Mondale	8%	(36,237 votes)

Ventura for Governor 1998

Election Industry, Inc. never saw Jesse Ventura coming. His upset victory in the 1998 Minnesota governor's race was an outcome that the pollsters, pundits, and party hacks that make up Election Industry, Inc. couldn't have predicted, capping an election that slipped out of their control. Washington forces don't like it when an election ventures beyond what they can manipulate, explain, or even understand. It makes their polls purposeless, their fundraising schemes useless, their elaborate political science theories helpless. Worst of all, it makes them look stupid.

But there is something we should all like about unlikely political upsets: they are proof that democracy can still remain in the hands of the voters.

I'll admit that even I was surprised by Ventura's victory—by Election Day I had already analyzed the factors and had determined they would leave him just short of winning. Though

I was encouraged by reports of high voter turnout on Election Day, a reporter leaked to me an early exit poll that had Ventura at only 31 percent, trailing Humphrey and Coleman at 34 percent each. I had thought he would ultimately finish at 29 percent or 30 percent, tops.

We were not going to win, but we had come close. As I headed out to the site of the evening's party, I was at peace. I could honestly tell the press that all of us in the campaign had reason to be very proud of ourselves, and I decided I would suggest that Jesse do so in his concession speech, too. With nothing else worthwhile to do until the polls closed, I decided to get a head start on my customary post-analysis.

Post-analysis notes written 11/3/98 (Election Day)
RE: Jesse Ventura for Governor, Reform Party, Minnesota

This campaign has accomplished more with less than any major campaign in the history of the state of Minnesota. The people involved, from the candidate to every single Ventura voter, have nothing to hang their heads about.

Jesse didn't win because the campaign lacked party support from what is supposed to be a major political party. A great candidate can only do so much on his own. At a certain point, the party apparatus has to take over and deliver what it can for the candidate. The Reform Party isn't there yet.

You could not have asked more of Jesse Ventura as a candidate. He exceeded expectations at every juncture. There is no more he could have done. Like he is portrayed in some of his movies, he is a warrior. I would go into battle with him anytime.

We were inundated in the final 36–48 hours by the hugest barrage of advertising I've ever personally witnessed. I monitored TV coverage of the race from Friday forward. . . . Seeing it entirely from the voters' perspective is a mortifying experience. With such an incessant amount of inane crap on the air, it's a wonder anybody still bothers to vote for *anyone.*

If we get every Republican and Democratic vote we targeted, plus all the independents, we still probably top out at 29%, 30, 31 at best, and that's not enough. Of course, if we can get to 31%, it's not that far to 33. And at 33%, in a three-way race, if it's as close as they say—anything can happen.

Hours later, I was reminded that anything could indeed happen. By midnight, all three networks called the race for a stunned Jesse Ventura. He had won the biggest election upset in the country, in the state's history, maybe even in the last century of American politics. As he would put it moments later, borrowing from his hero, Muhammad Ali: "We shocked the world!"

It had been only six weeks since I first considered the possibility of working for Ventura's gubernatorial campaign. My candidate in the DFL primary had lost to Attorney General Skip Humphrey, and the governor's race was ramping up to predictable form. The major-party candidates had already fully embraced the campaign tactics of Election Industry, Inc.; both Humphrey and the Republicans' Norm Coleman, mayor of St. Paul, were embarking on a spending frenzy, fueled by taxpayer's public campaign financing dollars and soft money expenditures directed by the state Republican and DFL parties. By mid-September, Election Industry, Inc. was already in high gear.

But there was palpably something in the air, something that I hadn't sensed since the 1990 Wellstone win. People were looking for something different, for another choice. Jesse's campaign was already the most interesting third party venture since Perot's 1992 campaign, so I contacted Ventura campaign chairman Dean Barkley and we immediately began exploring whether we could work effectively together.

Barkley was a 1996 U.S. Senate candidate whose 7 percent of the vote helped secure Paul Wellstone's second term while maintaining major-party status for the Reform Party in Minnesota. Dean had spent two years recruiting Ventura, who ran as an Independent when he was elected mayor of Brooklyn Park, Minnesota—his only previous elected office. On the first Friday night of October, Barkley suggested I come to the TV studio to watch Jesse in action, figuring I would be impressed at Ventura's prowess in debating the Republican and Democratic nominees. I wasn't prepared to be all that impressed, but I was. Like Perot, Jesse let himself be himself on the debate platform, where many a candidate has allowed the high stakes to lead them to try to be more than themselves. He made an immediate connection with the audience that his competitors couldn't begin to approach.

Then came the most amazing moment I have ever seen in any televised political debate.

The moderators were attempting to pin down the candidates on a particularly tricky issue: the Defense of Marriage Act. In the 1996 U.S. Senate race, Paul Wellstone had enraged his many gay and lesbian supporters by saying he supported such legislation, which outlawed giving long-time gay partners the same legal rights that spouses had. Coleman, of course, reassured his conservative supporters by stating his strong approval of the legislation. Humphrey talked over, under, and around the issue before saying he probably supported it more so than not.

Then Jesse told a moving story about two gay friends of his, longtime partners living together, one of whom ended up in the hospital with a critical illness. The sick man's partner visited the hospital and cared for his bedridden mate every day—every day, that is, until the sick man's estranged family showed up. The family never would accept the fact that their son and brother was gay, and had effectively disowned him many years before. Now they were at the hospital to take over making the decisions about how this man would be cared for before—and after—he died. Worse, as the patient slipped into a coma, the family withdrew permission for his gay partner to visit, blocking him from his longtime partner's bedside. Ventura argued that denying gay people these normal rights and using the law in this way was not only morally reprehensible, it was an unnecessary intrusion of government into people's private lives.

When he arrived at the moral of his story, jaws dropped all across the state, mine possibly furthest of all. "Love," he said, "is bigger than government."

Like everyone else, I had anticipated nothing like this from the macho ex-Navy SEAL and former pro wrestler. Here was a candidate whose next move no one would be able to predict, especially the chronically backward-looking stalwarts of Election Industry, Inc. The rest of this campaign was going to be a wild-card conversation no one could control.

That sealed it for me. "I want to work with this guy," I told Barkley. With Election Day less than four weeks away, we signed on to the most amazing twenty-four-day ride any campaign would ever see.

I knew that victory would come only as an unbelievable upset against incredible odds. But we had done it before. And like Paul Wellstone in 1990, Jesse Ventura was the true populist in this race. But unlike the 1990 version of Paul Wellstone, Jesse Ventura is larger than life. He had strong name identification and a well-established persona, and the invaluable ability to communicate in the kind of common, everyday language that strikes voters as personal and down-to-earth. Finally, like Wellstone eight years earlier, nobody expected him to win, so he had nothing to lose by telling the truth. The result: people believed whatever he said, a trait that is money in the bank for a media consultant.

I can't say that either Jesse or I ever expected him to win, but upon doing our targeting analysis, I knew it was at least a possibility. The primaries had revealed that neither of the two major party candidates had captured the public's imagination. Though at first glance Skip Humphrey looked like a prohibitive favorite in the general election—doubling his nearest competitor in a crowded primary field—there was another way to look at his 37 percent plurality: for 63 percent of the people voting in his own party's primary, he wasn't their first choice. Humphrey, I realized, wasn't the juggernaut everybody was saying he was.

One reason that the press, and others, considered Ventura such a long shot was their failure to comprehend the dynamics of a competitive three-way election.

Hung up on the idea it takes over 50 percent of the vote to win a general election, people and the press fool themselves into assuming that a third-party candidate cannot be competitive. But that's not the way the numbers work in a true three-way race, in which the winner needs only a plurality, not a majority. In this race, a candidate could win with as little as 34 percent of the vote, a message that we immediately had to get across—to the press, to the voters, and even to the campaign—in order to establish our credibility.

I felt I knew both the Republican and Democratic playbooks in this election as if I had written them myself. And I knew that their playbooks had nothing in them about how to run against a legitimate third-party candidate. Contrast was going to be key. Even though Skip and Norm were not very much alike, Jesse could make them seem similar in the public's mind by lumping them together as career politicians and tools of special interest groups. The more he did that, the better his chances of becoming the viable alternative.

Neither candidate believed that our core support was strong: they figured it was just a matter of time before people ended their flirtation with Jesse and broke one way or the other. Regardless, he would be controlling the swing votes that both candidates would need, which I was pretty certain would insulate him from attack by the other two candidates, fearful of alienating his supporters. But it is not in the nature of Election Industry, Inc. not to attack, so I was sure Coleman and Humphrey would go after each other. This would give Ventura another opportunity to contrast himself favorably— by staying above the fray, he could portray them as typical politicians resorting to typical attack politics.

Still, the day would come when Election Industry, Inc. and the major candidates would attempt to convince voters that Jesse couldn't win—and that a vote for Ventura would be a wasted vote. This was perhaps the most poisonous mind-set that we faced. If the press came to the conclusion that Jesse couldn't win, the media would cease to cover us and focus on the two "real" candidates. And we needed the media attention—we couldn't compete with the multimillions the other candidates were spending on advertising and other communications. We had to devise a way to avoid getting pushed off the front page all the way through Election Day, and especially in those critical final days.

All of this was on our minds as we assembled a comprehensive communications strategy in roughly a week's time. We identified where our base vote was—the people we absolutely had to have; where the opportunities were to pick up Democratic votes (mostly in working-class neighborhoods and towns just outside the metro area); and where we thought our Republican opportunities would be (in the suburbs). We plotted how to find those voters, get their attention, get their support, and then keep it. With voter targeting techniques as our secret weapon, we could direct Jesse's campaigning to prioritize the use of his time, focus our field and organizational efforts, and make our media buys much more efficient than the competition's.

Ever eager to see the future as a repeat of the past, Election Industry, Inc. predicted that Ventura's entry would help assure Humphrey's victory, in the same way Perot helped put Clinton in the White House in 1992. I suspected the party hacks were oversimplifying things—I knew we could pull away votes that both the Democrats and the Republicans were counting on. But I was convinced that our future rested not only with the undecided traditional voters that both sides were fighting over, but with voters beyond the range of their rifle scopes.

Undecideds are a misunderstood lot. Of the eligible voters who are actually expected to show up, there are plenty who don't make up their minds until a few weeks or even days before Election Day. The two major parties generally characterize undecided voters as procrastinators who are less interested in and less informed about politics; not surprisingly, we have seen over the years how wrong this prevailing wisdom can be. Though undecided voters are not all alike, I've learned that they do share some tendencies. Undecided voters are often more moderate and independent-minded, in contrast to the party loyalists who make up their minds early on. They usually aren't single-issue voters, who typically know which candidate is theirs pretty early in the race. Undecideds take their votes seriously, and take their time making their decisions. And they are often more interested in the candidate than in the issues.

More important, they are not reached by the traditional

channels of Election Industry, Inc. Undecideds tend to like to make their own decisions and are more distrustful of the press, they are less swayed by ads or by other people telling them what to do, and they like to search out their own sources of information (if they have the time) and do their own analysis. Many of them are "wired": people who spend a lot of time on a computer and on the internet, either at work or at home or both. These were people who, once identified, we could reach.

Weeks before Election Day 1998, voter turnout was forecast at roughly 50 percent. But what about the other half? Perot had demonstrated in 1992 that voters who disapproved of or had given up on the two major parties could be brought out to the polls. Yet the two major parties always ignore the infrequent and lapsed voters, as well as those who have never voted before. While Democrats and Republicans pay lip service to young people, their conventional wisdom holds that young people can't be counted on to vote, are hard to reach by mail or phone, and are driven by concerns more ideological than the bread-and-butter issues of traditional voters. They aren't predictable, so the major parties avoid expending time and energy on them, instead exploiting them as free volunteer labor to do the crap work that no one else wants to do.

I saw that Jesse had a special bond with young people. He thought differently from the status quo, like they did. He refused to pander to them, and he treated them seriously, even if he disagreed with their positions. And he spent time really listening to them and interacting with them.

It would be a risky strategy to focus solely on these opportunity audiences that other campaigns overlooked. But I knew we already had some of that 50 percent who were going to be voting. And I believed it was a better gamble to find more of that ignored 50 percent than to compete for the 50 percent constantly talked to by the other candidates' ads.

Both of the other campaigns were fixated on using their ad

budgets to attract the votes of women, apparently assuming that union men and fiscally conservative men were already safely in the folds of the Democrats and Republicans, respectively. That meant that they ignored a lot of television shows, generally programs for young people or men, on which we could advertise and have the stage to ourselves. Without a lot of media clutter, and with no rebuttal from the competition's ads, our message could take root outside the time slots that Election Industry, Inc. effectively controlled.

We would never be able to compete with their budgets, so our commercials would have to be produced cheaply, quickly, and with minimal demands on the candidate's vital campaigning time. But the last thing we could afford to be was boring. We had to make Jesse the talk of the state in a matter of days.

With so little money to spend, we were uncomfortably dependent on free media. Most of the media had covered Ventura's candidacy as a summer diversion, and were ultimately not going to take him seriously, fostering a general impression among the public that he was a sideshow, and not really a credible candidate. We were going to have to convince the media of his legitimacy as a candidate to build more credibility into the campaign.

The press, typically, was waiting to see money being spent on TV advertising before they would deem Jesse a candidate credible enough to cover seriously. We couldn't reach the levels of advertising spending that would get the press's attention—unless, I realized, we could make news out of our advertising. Fortunately, the imagination of the press was intrigued by the notion of Ventura's bravura combined with our creativity. They were expecting something different, and they were eager to cover it—especially since the other two candidates were running the usual kind of dull, conventional campaigns that come straight from the cookie cutters of Election Industry, Inc.

The media came out in force to the press conference where we unveiled our first commercial, "I Believe," a sixty-second spoken-word spot with patriotic music in which Jesse recited many of the reasons he was running. But he also voiced a number of his long-held personal beliefs, some of which were of a variety never before heard in a political ad. All it took was the sound of Jesse saying "I believe the Rolling Stones are the greatest rock 'n' roll band ever" to serve immediate notice that this was not going to be a predictable campaign.

We invited TV crews into the studio to film the recording of our next ad, one of the most outrageous political radio ads ever recorded. A testament to the power of music as a mnemonic device, "Jesse's Theme" featured a campy soul riff that reminded some people of Isaac Hayes' theme from "Shaft," with Jesse himself supplying some of the vocals. The news ran unforgettable footage of Jesse growling "I'm no career politician!" into a microphone while female vocals chanted "Jesse! Ventura!" and cooed "Oooh, Jesse!" in the background. After only a few airings, "Jesse's Theme" was one of the most requested songs on the radio, thanks to all the people who had heard about the song without—due to our paucity of media dollars—yet hearing the actual commercial.

The centerpiece of our ad strategy was a pair of TV commercials that defied expectations while maximizing the appeal of Jesse's unique persona. "Action Figure," born of an unconventional ad idea originally rejected by the conventional thinkers surrounding the 1996 Wellstone reelection campaign, featured a child playing with a custom-made Jesse Ventura action figure toy. It even set off a flood of calls to television stations and toy stores from parents looking for the nonexistent toy.

Without requiring any of his valuable campaigning time to be spent shooting the commercial, we had made Jesse once again a cult hero. Ventura approved the "Action Figure" concept within moments of seeing it; the other ad for which the campaign is so fondly remembered took some more convincing. "Jesse the Mind," taking its title from the candidate's own variation on his wrestling moniker, Jesse "The Body" Ventura, showed Jesse in statuesque contemplation—and in nothing but workout shorts—mimicking Rodin's nude thinker's pose. The camera angles and operatic soundtrack resembled anything but a political ad, softening Jesse's image while broadening his appeal, and portraying him as a candidate of substance.

By the final week of the campaign, it was clear that we were pulling support from both candidates. The debates had proved to be the perfect vehicle for Ventura to contrast himself against two "career politicians," pointing out that neither had ever held a private sector job, instead stuffing themselves at the public trough for their entire lives. The debates also pointed out Humphrey's and Coleman's major deficiencies—the former demonstrating that he was a far lesser version of his father, a candidate who looked better on paper than in person, while the latter tried too hard to be Kennedy-esque, and looked too slick.

Politically, both major party candidates were attempting the familiar post-primary Election Industry, Inc. move to the center, but they were surprised to find the political middle already occupied by Ventura. Still, the question that the media and Election Industry, Inc. continued to focus on was which side of the ledger he was going to hurt more. No one believed he could be perceived as centrist enough to attract a true plurality of the vote—especially with no money. As the final campaign weekend approached, the choruses of "Jesse can't win" from the press and pundits grew ever louder. But we were prepared to show them different.

To cap off his otherwise forgettable 1996 presidential campaign, Bob Dole had spent the last seventy-two hours of the race traveling nonstop around the country. At the time, I didn't quite understand the purpose of that trip. Was he trying to tell us he wasn't too old to be president? Was he trying to show us he could stay up late? But now, two years later, it occurred to me that a marathon campaign event would be the perfect vehicle for a former Navy SEAL.

This seventy-two-hour "Drive to Victory," as we dubbed it, would be a hard mission for even an experienced and well-trained campaign to accomplish. For a ragtag group of volunteers, it would be nearly impossible. There was little room for error. The press wouldn't ignore it, which was our whole intention, but it could backfire: if the campaign was ineffective in pulling it off, the negative stories would stamp out any chance we had of winning. Either the press would say "this is the group that we want to put in charge of our government?" (if there were numerous logistical breakdowns) or "Jesse really can't win" (if we didn't succeed in turning out crowds).

Following a route that our targeting data indicated would take us where we could pick up the most votes, the "Drive to Victory" drew crowds beyond our wildest expectations, leaving no doubt it was a risk that paid off. Even before it ever got started there were signs of its success, when both of the competition's campaigns paid us the supreme compliment of trying to imitate the idea. We announced the Drive to Victory at a press conference the Wednesday afternoon before Election Day, and immediately the other campaigns were scrambling to put together their own bus tours by the weekend. They drove around repeating their message of "Jesse can't win, so vote for me," but it rang increasingly hollow as images of huge crowds flocking to Ventura's Drive to Victory dominated the news.

The competition gave us one more publicity gift before

we even made it to our final Election Eve, get-out-the-vote rally—a typical eleventh-hour Election Industry, Inc. dirty trick that backfired in spectacular fashion. Coming out of a TV station after three days of nonstop campaigning, we found out about a last-minute mailer, a distortion of Ventura's positions on labor issues sponsored by some unions who wanted Humphrey to win. We called an immediate press conference in the station parking lot where Ventura, illuminated only by the lights of the TV cameras, reached into his wallet and pulled out his union card. Neither of the other candidates has ever been in a union, he pointed out, while noting that he and his lieutenant governor running mate, an elementary school teacher in her sixties named Mae Schunk, were both long-time union members. This gave us a priceless sound bite for all the stations' late news shows, and it was a late—but great—example of how the campaign was slipping further out of Election Industry, Inc.'s control.

Perhaps due to the exhaustion of the participants, many of whom had not stopped campaigning for three straight days—or perhaps due to the death threat Ventura received that night, forcing him to don a bulletproof vest before taking the stage—the election eve rally never became as electric as I had hoped. But we more than made up for it the following night at Canterbury Downs, a racetrack in the southwestern suburbs of Minneapolis.

At the racetrack, with its numerous TVs, the numbers that counted started arriving, slowly at first. Shortly after the polls closed at 8:00 p.m., Jesse came out of the gate with an early lead at 37 percent with 9 percent of the vote counted—too high to be true, I thought, it would have to come down. I had worked out a game plan for the evening: we would probably fall out of contention by 9:30 or 10:00, and I'd have to do a few live interviews, probably for the 10:00 p.m. news. Partly because of this, mostly as a superstition, I told myself I would not have a drink until we fell behind, which ought to be as soon as the next set of numbers, surely by 9:00 p.m. or so.

Fifteen percent of the vote was tallied, and he was still leading the pack: Jesse 37, Skip 32, Norm 30.

We didn't have any runners in the field or people to feed us vote totals from the precincts, so I tried to hunker down in front of the four TV screens in the private backstage party room to concentrate and get some information. The room was reserved for the campaign brain trust (all three or four of us), and the Ventura family and friends. That night there were a lot more family and friends than brain trust, and they were a raucous crowd totally oblivious to the TVs. Rowdy as the backstage partiers were, they were nothing compared to the crowd in front of the stage, where the hard-core Jesse voters were body surfing without any music. Every time a live TV report came on, the place turned into a mosh pit.

The vote totals were adding fuel to the merriment. Nobody really thought they were going to hold up, but everyone was sure having fun, realizing we were scaring the hell out of the other two candidates.

Thirty-four percent of the vote in, a third around the track: Jesse 37, Norm 32, Skip 30.

One station cut to a live report from Humphrey's campaign. I knew all the people in range of the camera, and to a person, they looked like somebody just ran over their dog. How could that be, I thought? Humphrey's people have much better information than we do.

Humphrey's campaign manager was on camera, trying to explain his 30 percent number. He was claiming confidence that their numbers would start to move once the metro returns came in, but his face was saying something else entirely.

Wait a minute, I thought. The metro returns are always the

first to come in. If Democrats weren't projecting those traditionally Democratic metro precincts for Skip, who was getting them? It couldn't be Norm, could it?

Thirty-eight percent counted: Jesse 37, Norm 33 (making his move!), Skip 30.

I had begun trying to think how I could construct a feasible explanation for my press interviews. Well, I suppose Norm could be getting a lot of St. Paul votes. He *is* the mayor of St. Paul, reelected as a Republican in a Democratic city. But in truth, I didn't understand these numbers.

Forty-four percent in: 37/33/30. Like a racehorse intent on running wire to wire, Jesse refused to give any ground. He opened at 37, he was still at 37.

A live report from the Republican victory party showed a crowd that looked less shattered than Skip's party, but not by much. Maybe they couldn't understand how Skip could be so low without them being in the 40s, or awfully close.

Fifty-five percent of the vote counted, more than halfway home: Jesse 37, Norm 34 (closing in!), Skip 28.

Wow. This was turning into a long night, much longer than anybody had anticipated. None of the stations was projecting a winner, and they always tried to beat each other to the punch just as soon as they could.

With 60 percent of the vote in, we were coming up on the home stretch, and there was still no change. The crowd by then had doubled, and then doubled again, people streaming into Canterbury Downs like it was the best party on earth. Even the State Patrol had arrived—to keep order and direct traffic, I thought. By this point it was well after 11:00 p.m. and time for Jesse to say something to the crowd, especially as big and loud as it was getting. The family party room was so massively packed I couldn't move, no one could hear, and I couldn't even see the TV sets that very few revelers were paying attention to. It reminded me of the one Kentucky Derby I attended—we were in the infield, and through the entire race card, I never saw a horse, until I caught the briefest glimpse of Seattle Slew. I got one quick glance at a TV screen—Jesse was still at 37, running with the heart of a champion, refusing to yield—then looked over at the candidate, whose big bald head was bobbing above a sea of friends and family members.

Suddenly the room erupted. People were screaming and pointing at the TV screen. The CBS station had just projected Jesse Ventura as the winner! Ventura was looking around and bellowing my name, trying to locate me. I was the only one with experience in matters like this, the only one in the room who had been here before, the only so-called expert in this ragtag, revolutionary campaign.

"Hillsman! They can't do that, can they?" Ventura asked me. "I'm not going out there with just 60 percent of the vote counted to claim victory. I'm not going to look like a jackass when they're wrong."

I told him that they were usually not wrong about these things, but to be certain, we could just stay backstage and wait for another station to call it. Sure enough, inside of a minute, another checkmark went up next to his name. Unfortunately, it was the local independent station, not a network affiliate. Ventura's noggin jerked in my direction again, like a hooked fish.

I shrugged and smiled weakly. "Uh, that's the local station. That's more like *half* a checkmark."

We didn't have to wait much longer to make history. Within moments, with nearly 70 percent of the returns in, ABC and NBC also called it for Ventura. Now I got to break the news. "It's for real. You won. You're the governor-elect of the state of Minnesota."

Jesse Ventura had won the biggest political upset in the country. Amid the pandemonium, Jesse, his wife Terry, campaign manager Doug Friedline, campaign chair Dean Barkley, myself and a few others wedged ourselves into a closet-sized anteroom to figure out what to say to the crowd and to the press. Jesse and Terry both looked stunned.

Terry's cell phone rang. It was Maria Shriver, calling from NBC. Her husband, Arnold Schwarzenegger, was one of Jesse's Hollywood buddies, and the two couples were close friends. But right now she was calling not just with congratulations, but to make sure NBC's Tom Brokaw got the first national interview with Jesse, at midnight Central time. About ten minutes away.

As Jesse and his family went to the stage, the State Patrol took over protection detail from Ventura's volunteer security force. That's when I finally put two and two together: the State Patrol is charged with safeguarding the governor-elect, from the moment he is elected. They knew something I didn't, and they weren't here just to direct traffic.

I stood nearby on the periphery, watching the happiest and strangest-looking amalgam of voters I had ever seen. People from all walks of life, from every income level, in every kind of dress imaginable. People, I was certain, who almost never voted, who hated what politics had become.

It was the people's revenge against Election Industry, Inc.

Jesse's initial remarks were brief. Besides telling the assemblage that we shocked the world (indeed, we had!), Jesse said he would have more to say, but right now he had to make his way back to the riser with the TV cameras. He gangwayed his way through the crowd, and just as the clock struck midnight, he was standing in front of NBC's camera on national TV as the governor-elect of Minnesota and the first Reform Party candidate ever to be elected to high office.

The rest of the night was a whirlwind of press activity. The media was desperate to talk to the governor-elect, but while he was tied up, they were looking for anyone legitimately connected to the campaign who could shed some light on how and why this happened. At one point in the wee hours I was doing an interview for public radio with big honking headphones over my ears, and I looked across to see Barkley about twenty feet away, also talking into a radio reporter's microphone. Our eyes met while we were both listening to our next question, and all we could do was grin.

I never did get to have my first drink of the night, so I was stone cold sober when I left the racetrack after 3:30 a.m. My route home took me past a small commuter airfield. As I approached it, I noticed small planes landing, one after another. It was nearly four o'clock in the morning, and it looked like rush hour at O'Hare Airport.

The planes were carrying national media people who were told to get themselves to Minnesota at once to try to figure out what just happened, and to shed some light on this biggest political story in decades, which no one saw coming.

Once the finish line had been crossed and the numbers were all in, I could see how well our strategy had played out. The Ventura campaign was responsible for nearly 300,000 new voters taking part in the election. Voter turnout was eight percentage points higher than projected: 61 percent (2,124,630 voters) compared to an expected 53 percent (1,845,990). According to exit polls, 12 percent of all voters would not have voted if Ventura had not been in the race.

In Washington, no one can hear the people scream—even with joy, as they do when a Paul Wellstone or a Jesse Ventura wins. The clanking of Election Industry, Inc.'s political machinery and the continuous yammering of the punditry drowns it all out. But we had seen, once again, that when voters have someone to vote for as well as something to vote against, the political firmament can—and will—be shaken.

Tale of the Tape

Minnesota 1998 Gubernatorial General Election

Jesse Ventura (Reform)	37%	(772,285 votes)
Norm Coleman (R)	34%	(712,708 votes)
Hubert H. Humphrey III (DFL)	28%	(580,008 votes)
Projected voter turnout:	53%	(1,845,990 votes)
Actual voter turnout:	61%	(2,124,630 votes)

15% of all voters registered at the polls on Election Day. 12% of all voters would not have voted had Ventura *not* been in the race.

According to exit polls:

- Ventura received 39% of the male vote in the election and 34% of the female vote. His 39% tied Coleman among male voters and his 34% was only 2 points behind Humphrey among women. Humphrey got only 20% of the male vote.
- Ventura carried all age groups except sixty-plus (Coleman and Humphrey tied with 38% of this demographic segment). He had a 30-point lead over Humphrey among voters 18–29 and a 20-point lead over Humphrey in the largest age group (30–44).
- Ventura carried all income levels except those making over $100,000 a year, which Coleman carried.
- Ventura carried voters who were high school graduates and those who had some college. He

trailed Coleman by 3 points among college graduates.

- Ventura captured 33% of voters who identified themselves as Democrats, 29% of those who identified themselves as Republicans, and 52% of independents. He tied with Humphrey among liberals (44%) and carried the moderates by a wide margin (8 points over Humphrey, 11 points over Coleman).
- He carried both the people who felt their personal financial situation was going to get worse (by 20 points, 51/31 over Coleman) and those who felt it would get better (with 38%, 6 points over Coleman and 8 points over Humphrey).
- Among people who disapproved of Congress's performance, Ventura carried 40% (Humphrey carried 31% and Coleman 27%).
- Ventura carried 35% of the people who voted for Clinton in 1996, 25% of the people who voted for Dole, and a whopping 76% of the people who voted for Perot. Most remarkably, Ventura carried 63% of the voters who did not vote in the 1996 presidential election, either because they were too young or because they didn't like their choices. He captured 35% of the people who supported Clinton in 1998, 27% of those who opposed Clinton, and 40% of the people in the middle.
- Ventura's strength was pronounced among moderates. He carried 33% of the people who felt Clinton should be impeached and 34% of the people who felt Clinton should resign, and at the same time took 39% of those who felt

Clinton shouldn't be impeached, and 40% of those who believed he should not resign. He carried 40% of the people who approved of Clinton's job performance and 43% of the people with a favorable image of Clinton as a person. But he also carried 32% who didn't like the way Clinton was doing his job, and 35% of those who viewed him negatively as a person.

- More people who thought Clinton should not be censured voted for Ventura than voted for the Democrat in the race (42% Ventura, 33% Humphrey).

- He carried 36% of the voters who felt the state's economy was excellent, 36% of those who thought it was good, and 52% of the people who thought it was not good.

- Ventura more than doubled each of his two opponents' support among people who felt the economy and jobs was the most important issue facing the state, and among those who felt crime and drugs was the most important issue facing the state.

- Most telling for the future of nonpartisan politics, Ventura captured 94% of the votes from people who would have sat out the election if their only two choices were Coleman and Humphrey. Showing that he truly did draw from both parties, 29% of Ventura voters would have voted for Coleman if only the Republican and the Democrat were in the race, and 28% would have voted for Humphrey.

Secrets of
Three-Breakfast Polling

I don't believe in polling. But I do believe in research.

And having worked on any number of underfunded campaigns that can't afford to do quantifiable research, I've figured out all sorts of cheap ways to divine what people are thinking.

I was trained to be an advertising copywriter. One of the first things you learn as an advertising copywriter is this: you do not miss deadlines. If you do, and there's no ad to run in the space that was bought, the money comes out of your pocket.

Copywriters, like all writers, hate deadlines and will do anything to put off starting to write. They are full of excuses. One of the biggest excuses is, "I don't have enough information" or "I'm waiting for the research."

Well, sometimes the research never comes. But you still have to write an ad.

An old journalism professor of mine told me what to do in those situations. He called it "the hat trick," because it went back to the days when men wore hats (and copywriters were men).

You put on your hat, walked out the door, and like any good reporter, dug up the information for yourself.

Maybe you'd get some of it from the library. Maybe you'd get some of it by talking to customers or buyers. Maybe you'd get insights by visiting the plant where the product was made, or by talking to the people who made it.

Maybe you'd just sit and observe as people picked up the product, put it down, or bought it. Maybe you'd talk to the salespeople. Maybe you'd buy it and try it yourself. Maybe you'd drive around and count the number of them in service.

Maybe you'd do all these things. But at the end of the day, you wouldn't still be waiting in your office for something to happen. And you would be in a much better position to begin creating the ad.

With politics, it's even easier. I can go into any city in the United States, and within a day or two, I can have a very good sense of what the people in that city are thinking and what the key issues in the election are.

All you have to do is read the local papers—the more of them, the better; and the more local, the better. Not just dailies, but the alternative weeklies, the neighborhood papers, the free papers. Listen to local talk radio shows. Watch the local news and some of the local TV shows.

Then get out and drive around the area. Pay attention. Observe. Listen.

You'll notice I haven't said "talk to people." Talking to people is good, but there area a lot of areas in the country where people don't cotton to strangers asking them a bunch of questions like some amateur pollster. They might be polite, but they may not tell you what they really think. Talking to people is good, but listening to them is even better.

And eavesdropping is best of all.

During Paul Wellstone's 1990 campaign, each week I would take the Sunday paper and go to three different cafes. I would go alone, sit there, eat, and pretend to read the paper. But what I'd really be doing is listening to conversations.

We went into the final weekend trailing by 5–7 points in the latest newspaper polls. After going to three cafes in three different parts of the Twin Cities on Saturday, and doing the same thing on Sunday, I didn't know if we were going to win, but I did know we were going to do awfully well in the core metro area.

In the final month of Jesse Ventura's campaign, I used this strategem to figure out whether our ads were getting noticed or not, and which ones people were talking about the most. For the first three weeks of October, all we could afford were radio ads. I would listen to people mention the ads, then I'd go back and change the rotation of the ads for the next week. I didn't have poll data, but I could tell which ads were working better than others.

It's amazing all the useful information you can find out in these kinds of situations, assuming you're picking the right cafes. You can find out how your candidate is doing. You can find out if your ads are working. You can find out which issues are really on people's minds. You can get a good sense for how many people are going to come out to vote.

I call it "three-breakfast polling." It can be lonely—you pretty much have to do it by yourself, or whoever you're with will distract you from your purpose. It's not scientific—it gives pollsters apoplexy—and it's not good for your cholesterol count. But at the same time it's expanding your waistline, it broadens your mind and your thinking.

There are other cheap ways of gauging voter reaction, too. If one of your commercials ever comes on TV in a crowded place, look for the reaction of the crowd. They might not be able to hear it. But look at their faces. If they can see it, if they are familiar with it from previous airings, you can pick up some clues as to its effectiveness. (Hint: A blank stare is not good. Poking another person and pointing to the TV screen is good.)

Nearly every campaign, no matter how ill-funded, will have volunteers making get-out-the-vote phone calls, especially in the final weeks of the campaign. These volunteers can be a wealth of information. Talk to them. Ask them what people are saying: about the candidate, about the issues, about the ads, about the news. Again, it's not scientific. But it can be awfully enlightening.

So if you see me dining alone, reading the paper, and looking overfed, don't cry for me. I'm working.

My Dinner with
Warren and Annette

There were many progressive Democrats who were none too thrilled with the cast of Democratic politicians angling to run for president in 2000.

One of them was named Warren Beatty.

Early in August of 1999, the political columnist Arianna Huffington called me to say she was faxing me a draft of an upcoming column of hers, urging Warren Beatty to run for president. She wanted to know, what did I think of the idea?

I told her I thought both political parties were more interested in holding on to power than they were in addressing and solving the country's problems. I told her that I thought the Democratic Party was controlled by a group of dangerous moderates, with Dick Morris as their Rasputin and the polling firm Penn & Schoen—better they should use the comedy team Penn & Teller!—as their two-headed but blind Tiresias (Arianna is well-versed in Greek mythology). I told her that the Democrats were on a path where whatever happened to assuage white suburban soccer moms at the moment seemed to define the party's current agenda.

I told her that any challenge to this retarded thinking would not come from high-profile elected officials within the party but would have to come from concerned Democrats outside the royal court of Election Industry, Inc. I told her getting Democrats to address real issues in the presidential primary could only happen if someone well-known, rich enough, and brave enough took on the task—the challenge had dwarfed even a sitting U.S. senator like Paul Wellstone.

I told her I liked the idea a lot. So she invited me to come to dinner at her house and meet Warren Beatty.

Warren Beatty is one of my four favorite actors (along with Clint Eastwood, Robert DeNiro, and Jack Nicholson), and I figured anybody brave or crazy enough to make the movie *Bulworth* is brave and crazy enough to take on the Democratic establishment. So I was excited to arrive at Arianna's small dinner party, but disappointed to find the guest of honor missing. He was sick.

Midway through the dinner, I was surprised to receive a phone call, the first of many from a man who uses the phone as deftly and regularly as Tiger Woods uses his short irons. "Bill, Warren is on the phone," Arianna purred in her charming-but-hard-for-a-Midwesterner-to-decipher Greek accent. "He wants to speak to you."

Even on the phone, Warren Beatty is the coolest guy in the room.

Hello?

Bill? This is Warren Beatty. Sorry I couldn't be there. I have some kind of bug that's knocked me flat. He sounded terrible. **What are you doing tomorrow?**

Uh, nothing.

Why don't you give me a call in the morning? Maybe we can get together then, around 10:30 or 11:00.

Uh, OK.

And he was on to his next phone call.

I went back to the table, and, after a delightful conversation with Arianna's brilliant Greek mother that went far into the night, I left and went to my hotel.

The next morning I called the Beatty residence. Warren got on the phone and was barely audible.

Did you ever have green tea?

He sounded even worse than the night before.

What?

Did you ever have green tea? I've got laryngitis, but I've been drinking green tea, and I really think it's making me better.

Actually, I drank a lot of green tea growing up—especially if I was sick—and still do today. Most of the time it's Lipton, not the fancy blend I suppose they drink in Beverly Hills, but I was not unaware of the healing powers of green tea. I told him so.

Whatever the restorative powers of the particular green tea he was drinking, he sounded much worse than the night before, more like he was stumbling down the footpath to death's door than on the road to recovery.

What are you doing later today? I really think I'm going to be better.

Uh, I'm doing whatever you want me to be doing. I came out here to see you, remember.

Call me later this afternoon, around three or so. Maybe we can get together tonight.

OK. Click.

I called back at 3:30.

What are you doing tonight? I can feel myself getting better.

Uh, nothing.

Why don't you come over for dinner? The help is off, so it's just me and Annette and the kids. I can't promise anything fancy, but maybe we can slip out somewhere and grab a bite, or order in. How about around seven?

Cool. I'm going to dinner with Warren Beatty. I got the address and said,

I'm there.

Beatty wore a white T-shirt, blue jeans and sneakers. For a man on the cusp of sixty, he had a waist that was about half his age. We should all look so bad when we are sick. He sounded pretty good, too. The green tea had worked.

Over take-out Chinese food and more green tea, we had about as stimulating, thorough, and well-informed a political conversation as I have ever had. It was clear that Warren Beatty was not another Trump-on-a-stunt.

Those people who know Beatty will tell you he makes decisions with all the speed of a runaway glacier. In this couple, he was by far the more careful. His wife, Annette Bening, is whip-smart, fully informed, and totally committed to doing whatever she and her husband can do as parents and as people to change the world for the better, to make it a better place for their children, for your children, and for mine.

When the discussion turned to making the decision whether or not to run, she seemed more passionate and inclined toward it than the reluctant candidate himself. I told them that I couldn't even begin to have an opinion about something so personal and so complicated, but that first and foremost they should consider the effect a campaign would have on their children and their marriage. Campaigns are not easy on candidates or families, no matter how wealthy or famous the candidate might be.

Beatty brought up his public image and whether that would be a problem. I said I didn't think so: if Clinton ran again for president he would be elected in a walk, and the American public seemed to have adopted a more mature and European view about the private lives of their elected officials.

"The public really doesn't know that much about me," he said. "They probably think I'm some kind of hedonist or libertine because I've been involved with a lot of different women. But I've never committed adultery. I've never taken drugs. And I don't drink. Not many people know me that well, but those who do will tell you—I'm a control freak. That's why I don't drink or mess around with drugs. I don't like being out of control."

I've heard much worse skeletons in the closet, let's put it that way.

The meeting with Beatty was interesting, but I didn't see him leaving the Democratic Party to run as an Independent—

certainly he had done nothing to indicate that. So I was a little surprised to get a call the next day from Patrick Caddell. A friend of Beatty's, Pat wanted me to meet with him over lunch at the Warner Brothers commissary. Pat, who was one of the whiz kids who got Jimmy Carter elected in 1976, was an adviser to the new TV series *The West Wing*. The show was filming its first-year episodes on the Warner Brothers lot.

Pat has consulted with many Democratic candidates at the highest levels of politics, but he is as sick of big-money politics and the two-party duopoly as I am. And he is exceptionally brilliant about politics, but once he gets going, it's hard for people of normal intelligence (like me) to keep up. We had a far-ranging conversation about whether a Beatty candidacy was viable. I thought it was, but funding the campaign could be problematical. Certainly Beatty could attract a significant amount of money, but raising the $25–50 million he would probably need to be competitive was a pretty tall task.

Caddell had a solution: we would go to the American public and tell them that we can reclaim our politics from the big-money interests . . . but it was going to cost them. Specifically, it would cost each American a hundred dollars and a hundred hours. If Beatty ran, we would ask every concerned American to donate $100 to the campaign, but more importantly, also contribute 100 hours of volunteer time to the campaign.

"I gotta believe there are at least half a million Americans in this country who would pay $100 to get their government back," Caddell said.

I wasn't so sure. A hundred dollars is a lot of money for most people in this country, especially for the people who suffer most at the hands of Election Industry, Inc. and its big money, special interest politics. But Pat's math was good. A half a million people giving a hundred dollars would amount to $50 million—puny for a national campaign for president, but even if it were half that, with smart targeting, the right message, and good communications, we could be a major factor.

I told Pat that I thought our work could amplify campaign budgets by a factor of one-and-a-half to three. That is, on the low end we can make a campaign's dollar worth $1.50 by being smart and creative about targeting, media buying, message, and communications. On the high end, we can make our clients' money worth three times that of the competition. And in extraordinary situations, even more: Wellstone spent less than half a million dollars in media and beat an incumbent Republican who spent between $6 and $8 million. Ventura spent less than $400,000 in media and beat a couple of major party candidates who between them and their sympathetic special interest "independent expenditures" spent upwards of $12 million. And in one of our most successful and cost-effective campaigns—where we took the side of the Air Line Pilots Association in their 1998 strike against Northwest Airlines— we were outspent nationally by about $53 million.

So I said to Pat we would be singularly unintimidated going up against the other Democrats and Election Industry, Inc.—candidates who might spend up to $100 million or more. Our work would be better and it would be more effective. But you can't go in with a peashooter and expect to outdo cannons. In every campaign, there is a critical mass that has to be reached in order to get your message out. For a major party's presidential primary, I calculated the minimum would range between $10 million and $25 or $30 million. At those spending levels, we would have a chance.

The Huffington column ran and the response was quick and encouraging, giving more credence to the notion that people were far from satisfied with the current field. Arianna's website, www.ariannaonline.com, received hundreds of emails, including many offers of $100 contributions to the campaign. Websites popped up to promote a Beatty candidacy, and one site received over one thousand emails and thousands of hits in little over a week. And, of course, the media—from newspapers to opinion columnists to talk shows to entertainment shows—were insatiable in their desire to find out something, anything, about a Beatty candidacy.

Obviously, Beatty wasn't making any comment. In the days following our dinner we spoke a couple of times (over the phone, naturally) about his entering the race, and about the nascent presidential campaign of one of his friends, John McCain (who had been their weekend guest just a few days before our dinner). But it was apparent Warren hadn't made any decision yet, and he wasn't going to make it anytime soon.

There was speculation in the national press after our meeting that I was sent as an emissary by Ventura to attempt to talk Beatty into running for president as an independent or a Reform Party candidate. That's not true. First of all, Ventura didn't even know about my trip until he heard about it in the media after the fact. Secondly, while Warren Beatty's politics and Jesse Ventura's politics may intersect at certain points, they don't intersect at very many points.

As early September came around, and more people were paying attention to something other than summer vacations, I worked up an idea for Beatty to tape a video press release. It would inform people that he had made no decision yet, but explain the reasons why he was considering running. It would get the message out to people that they *weren't* hearing the candidates talk about some pretty important problems, and at the same time put pressure on the leading candidates to stop ignoring these issues and get them into the national debate.

This is what I suggested he say to people:

My Dinner with Warren and Annette

Hi. I'm Warren Beatty.

A number of months ago I produced a movie in which I played a politician brave enough—or crazy enough—to tell Americans the truth about our government and politics.

Doing that movie caused me to really think about where our country is at today and where it is headed.

As many of you know, I'm no stranger to politics. I've been involved in presidential campaigns going back to Bobby Kennedy's in 1968.

Like most of you, I'm married now. My wife and I have three young children. They say having children changes people's lives. It certainly changed mine.

Now, every day my wife and I worry about our kids and the kind of country they'll grow up in. I'm sure you're concerned about it as well.

Before he was killed, Bobby Kennedy used to say, "Some people see what is and say 'why?' Others see what can be and ask 'why not?' "

That's what I find myself asking about our country, when our two major political parties are completely dominated by money and special interest groups. When we live in the richest nation in the world, yet 20 percent of our children are living in poverty. When our health is in the hands of insurance companies and not our family doctors.

That's why I'm considering running for president.

I'll be the first to say there has to be a better candidate for president than me. But so far, there's not a candidate in the race willing to tell the truth about these and the many other important problems facing us. So until somebody better shows up, I'm seriously considering giving it a shot.

We can change things if we do it together. With

enough people willing to donate just $100, or 100 hours of their time—or both—we could stop the influence of big money on politics and take back our democratic system from special interest groups.

I'm an actor. I like being an actor. Lord knows I don't need to be president (even though a lot of Americans would say the last actor we had as president didn't do such a bad job). And if I ever did become president, I would serve only one term, to get the country and the Congress's attention focused on what we *should* be paying attention to.

Then I'd go back to the private sector. I think that's pretty much the way our Founding Fathers wanted public service to be.

Some people will say I'm just using my celebrity. I don't dispute that. If it takes a certain kind of messenger to deliver the right message, so be it. I'm well aware of the criticisms. And I'm ready to stop considering this as soon as somebody better comes along.

(SUPER E-MAIL ADDRESS OR WEBSITE OR TOLL-FREE NUMBER)

Let me know what you think. Annette and I would appreciate your thoughts. (SMILES) Even if it's the names of candidates who'd be better than me.

In the end, Warren Beatty didn't run for president. In the campaign that followed, most of his and Annette Bening's questions about our country were scarcely asked, and certainly never answered. And if anybody took back our democratic system from the special interest groups, they did so without me—or anyone else—noticing.

Warren Beatty and Annette Bening are not politicians. They're concerned voters, just like me and you (assuming—hoping—that you still vote whenever you can find a candidate worthy of your vote). And like many of us, they saw that the system by which we elect our government was failing to produce a government that addresses our real concerns. They wanted to speak the same truth about our system that many of us want to say; they just had a better platform from which to speak it than the rest of us.

Speaking of platforms, if you want to hear the truth about how the Democrats and Election Industry, Inc. take some of their core constituencies for granted, go out tonight and rent *Bulworth.*

You'll laugh; you'll cry; you'll learn.

Presidential Follies

There were a lot of solid political reasons why an independent or third-party candidate could have won the presidency in 2000. Bill Clinton was term-limited, so an alternative candidate would not have to battle an incumbent. It was the new millennium, the year 2000—what better time, symbolically, for America to look beyond its two-party system? And the Democratic and Republican fields were looking weaker all the time. Nevertheless, the effort to find an independent or third-party candidate—the journey that would ultimately lead me to Ralph Nader and the Green Party—showed just how distressingly firm a hold Election Industry, Inc. has on our presidential elections.

I could already see a train wreck shaping up for the Reform Party. Though Ross Perot tended to treat the party as his private property, his claim had weakened considerably after the 1998 elections. By virtue of being the first Reform Party candidate to be elected to high office, Jesse Ventura was now the *de facto* leader of the party, at least in the eyes of independents and fans of new paradigm politics, as well as to the press and most political observers. Ventura was adamant that he had no interest in running for president in 2000, but I had still taken it upon myself to draft a secret presidential game plan—just in case. Especially given the low expectations Ventura would face, a 2000 run would show him what it took to put together and run a national campaign, and give the Reform Party its best shot at maintaining major party status with 5 percent of the vote. Not to mention positioning him for a real run at the White House in 2004, if that's what he chose to do.

I wasn't the only one contemplating a Ventura for President campaign. Shortly after the 1998 election, Frank Luntz and John Zogby released the results of a poll that the Republican Party had commissioned to try to understand the Ventura phenomenon and use it to their candidates' advantage. Luntz's recommendations were not remarkable, and probably impossible for most Republican candidates to implement: be the outsider, be modest and honest, use more out-of-the-box thinking, admit that you don't know everything, and (most incredibly) "assert [the Republican Party] as the true party of the people, not beholden to special interest groups or the Washington bureaucracy." This was not exactly practical advice.

What *was* remarkable were the numbers: nearly a third of the people surveyed nationally said they would consider voting for Ventura if he ran for president, and in a three-way race he polled 15 percent to Bush's 45 percent and Gore's 25 percent. Luntz noted correctly that "to get these kinds of numbers is extraordinary." Thinking back to where Jesse started in the polls in his race for governor, I thought to myself, it would certainly be a hell of a starting point, with plenty of time—over a year and a half—to election day.

Corroborating Luntz's double-digit starting point was a national poll done at the same time, commissioned by *Campaigns and Elections* magazine, which showed Ventura running noticeably stronger than Ross Perot at the top of a Reform Party presidential ticket. In this three-way race, Bush received 47 percent of the vote, Gore 33 percent, and Ventura 11 percent.

What the pollsters failed to recognize, as usual, is that they conducted the poll using only registered voters (usually Democrats or Republicans) and the sample size undoubtedly underrepresented political independents, nonvoters, lapsed voters, and first-time voters, all of whom would significantly expand Ventura's support.

Of course, all polls are especially specious this far away from an election, suitable only as fodder for conversation. And regardless of what any poll said, I knew that the chances of getting Ventura to run for president ranged from very slim to none, as were the odds of brokering any kind of rapprochement between the Perot loyalists in the Reform Party and the many party members who were dead-set against him. If the Reform Party was going to hold on to the major-party status Perot secured for it with his second presidential run in 1996, a candidate was needed that both Perot and Ventura and everyone else in the Reform Party could unequivocally stand up and salute.

The one candidate I knew everyone would salute was Colin Powell. I was convinced Powell could defeat any of the major-party candidates despite their advantages of financial and party support. But when Ventura's former campaign manager, Doug Friedline, and I finally made contact, Powell's representative spelled out two nonnegotiable reasons why a Powell for President campaign couldn't happen, at least not at this time. Despite appealing to the middle and being courted by both parties, Powell was and is a Republican, and could not possibly run against the presumed Republican candidate, George W. Bush—son of the president General Powell served under during the Gulf War. More importantly, Powell's wife Alma wouldn't let it happen, because she was convinced her husband would not be safe running for president. There's no arguing with that reasoning; it seems to me that no matter how far we have come as a country, our first black president might very well take office with a target on his back.

With Powell and Ventura out of the running, the anti-Perot Reform Party forces continued to search for a candidate as its July 1999 national convention drew ever closer. But it was clear not just to me that the Reform Party, the supposed third major party in America—with $13 million in public campaign funds—was drifting aimlessly towards the presidential election year.

Perot had saddled himself firmly on the fence, and refused to dismount. Every time it seemed like he was ready to take himself out of contention and move on to become the elder statesman of the party, he would look around at this organization he had bought, built, and paid for, and decide he wasn't quite ready to go out to pasture. Putting even more pressure on the party was speculation that Pat Buchanan, who was going nowhere in the Republican primary, saw a real opportunity to take over the Reform Party.

By mid-September of 1999, Buchanan had figured out that he was a dead man walking in the Republican Party presidential bazaar. For trained political operatives like the Buchanan people, the vacuum in the Reform Party made it a juicy, $13 million plum ripe for the picking. As Buchanan began making noises about quitting the Republican Party, his people plotted a petition drive and a 2000 convention strategy to take over the Reform Party for themselves. It seemed like an easy and logical target—Buchanan shared many of the themes that Perot had brought to the public's attention in 1992. But this would be no bloodless coup; for the avowed centrists in the Reform Party, it would be anathema to end up with "another party's castoff," as Ventura, the best trash-talker in politics (at least until retired NBA star Charles Barkley runs for office), described Buchanan. It would have to be a hostile takeover. And Pat Buchanan was certainly hostile enough to pull it off.

By this point, the Reform Party had splintered into five discernable blocs. First and still foremost were the Perotistas, continuing to hold out hope that their man would once again ride to the rescue even though he had shown no inclination to do anything of the sort. A second group was the realists among the former Perot supporters, who recognized the party would be radically changed to a right-wing conservative perspective if Buchanan took over. They became the basis for the "anyone but Buchanan" movement within the party. Ultimately, this group turned to the Natural Law Party's John Hagelin, though their support was tepid at best. Hagelin was seen as a last-resort placeholder whom they hoped could somehow maintain the Reform Party's major party status until it could get its act together before 2004.

The third group was the anti-Perot faction, who believed Perot had rigged his own nomination in 1996 and was certainly not the best candidate for the year 2000. As the loosely organized core of the Reform Party, they were the true centrists who largely embraced Jesse Ventura's brand of independent and populist politics. They were fiscal conservatives and social moderates, working people suspicious of big government and taxes, but also in favor of campaign finance reform, privacy issues, and true government by the people.

The American Reform Party had already split from the party after Perot's second run for president; his mercurial and authoritarian style had finally brought them to their breaking point. In many ways this was the most progressive wing of the party, true believers in a third path, in favor of anyone who could keep advancing a solid alternative party movement. Instead of waiting for some new savior to materialize, or getting behind the Hagelin push, this faction quickly endorsed Ralph Nader for president.

The last group, and by this time probably the largest, were the Buchanan supporters. Though their number also included some Reform Party loyalists willing to back Buchanan in an attempt to retain major party status with hopes of fighting and defeating him on another day, most of these people had come along with Buchanan from the Republican Party. They were a well-drilled group of ultra-conservatives who felt the Republican Party had gone too soft or moderate. They were isolationists, xenophobes, and populists in a conservative Christian sort of way. They were pro-morality, anti-abortion, and didn't see the need for trifling concepts like separation of church and state.

By early 2000, it was pretty obvious to careful observers that this last group could secure Buchanan the Reform Party nomination at that summer's convention. The Reform Party had always nominated its presidential candidate at a national convention where delegates had to be present to vote. The only way to stop Buchanan from seizing the 2000 convention, I reasoned, was to try something entirely new that would at the same time expand the party's reach: hold a virtual nominating convention.

I had met with the people who founded SpeakOut.com, an online, real-time polling facility whose technology could potentially be adapted for secure and accurate online balloting. We worked through some of the problems of cost, security, and registration, with an eye toward holding an open national primary online—expanding the membership of the Reform Party to such a degree that nearly anyone could vote. I was fairly certain we could get millions of people to register as Reform Party members just to participate in the nomination process. That way, millions of Americans could decide if Pat Buchanan was an acceptable Reform Party candidate for president, rather than a few hundred well-trained Republican imports, or a thousand or so delegates.

Of course, there was little doubt Ross Perot would place his name back in nomination if we did this, and I was fairly certain if that happened, he would win again. Still, I reasoned, better one more run by old Ross than having Buchanan hijack the party and take it in a completely different direction from where it was headed when it was founded.

But I also knew something else. If there was going to be any hope for a Jesse Ventura candidacy, a nationwide, internet-based balloting could serve as a draft mechanism that might pull him into the race as a last-minute, last-ditch candidate.

In the end, there wasn't enough time to pull it off, leaving the Reform Party only about eight months to find a candidate who could deprive Buchanan of the nomination. With no other candidate on the horizon, many eyes turned toward the carefully coiffed head of Donald Trump.

The Donald did nothing to discourage the speculation. He was certainly a match for Buchanan in braggadocio, and even showed up in Minnesota for an early 2000 Reform Party fundraiser. But Trump played to the press and said very little at the dinner, and I realized that this was all a publicity stunt; he was a salesman out to sell his latest book, not a candidate seeking votes.

Once the truth came out about Donald Trump, the handwriting was on the wall for Ventura and everyone else in the Reform Party to see. It was pretty obvious that the Reform Party presidential candidate would be either Pat Buchanan or Ross Perot, neither of whom was very appealing to Ventura or to the anti-Perot forces in the national Reform Party.

Ventura had had enough of the pro-Perot and anti-Perot

bickering within the party. He announced that he was forming a new party in Minnesota, the Independence Party, just fifteen months after becoming the first Reform Party member to
be elected to high office.

He was still not interested in running for president. The
Buchanan forces' takeover of the Reform Party was now virtually assured. But I had already been looking outside the Reform Party for months. In the buildup to the 2000 election, I
spoke with Independents, Democrats, even Republicans, before signing up with Ralph Nader to take on Election Industry,
Inc. in the first presidential election of the new millennium—
an election the Democrats seemed more hell-bent on giving
away with each passing month.

The Democratic presidential herd had been pretty well
thinned by the summer of 1999. After soapboxing that he
was "running to represent the Democratic wing of the Democratic Party," the one true progressive in the field, Paul Wellstone, dropped out by late 1998, citing health reasons. The
perennial Dick-Gephardt-for-President campaign had bless-
edly never materialized. Ted Kennedy had foregone his dreams
of the White House. Tom Harkin, who would have been stak-
ing out the same turf as Wellstone, had stepped aside to let
Paul tilt at the windmills this time. The Kerr(e)ys, John (Kerry)
and Bob (Kerrey), either decided their hour had not yet come
or they didn't want to rumble with such formidable opponents as Shufflin' Bill Bradley or Stormin' Al Gore. And Jesse
Jackson chose to stay on the sidelines instead of calling his
own number for his usual every-four-year play—a run around
the left end of the party. (I had suggested jokingly to people
that Wellstone and Jackson run together—a black and a Jew
running at the top of the ticket in 2000!—only to learn later
that Jackson and Wellstone actually *had* considered making

a Democratic primary run together, then dropped the notion when they couldn't agree on who would top the ticket).

Bradley, meanwhile, was attempting to wrap himself in the ill-fitting feather boa of Jesse Ventura. According to a *Wall Street Journal* article, the Bradley campaign was "stealing a leaf from the Ventura playbook, to turn out independents and younger, disaffected Americans who typically don't vote."

Yeah, right, I thought.

The herd mentality of Washington was lumbering once again. Ventura's campaign was the biggest political upset most political observers had witnessed in their lifetimes, and now the usual bandwagon-jumpers were obsessed with figuring out how to climb aboard the latest new thing and understand it well enough to bamboozle their clients.

This latest version of the emperor's new clothes is what makes the Election Industry, Inc. consultants so inept. Is there any living, breathing person outside of Washington, D.C. who does *not* see that Jesse Ventura and Bill Bradley are so fundamentally dissimilar in their personalities and their politics that it is ludicrous to attempt to convince people otherwise? Only Washington political consultants are dumb enough to think this is possible. It would be pitiful if it weren't so wasteful and so damaging to our politics.

Going from dumb to dumber, the Bradley campaign saw fit to go to the Democrats in Minnesota who were so badly beaten by Ventura in order to get advice on how to be more like him. This made about as much sense as asking someone who pots plants all day what is the best route to becoming an NFL Pro Bowl quarterback. I suppose it's remotely possible you could get some worthwhile advice, but it's not very likely.

The Bradley campaign's dealings with Election Industry, Inc. would astound me even further when I read a little later in the year that it had hired Anita Dunn as its main media consultant/strategist. Before joining Bradley's campaign, Ms. Dunn was one of the very top level executives in Squier Knapp Ochs Dunn, a longtime Democratic political consulting firm in Washington. What's so strange? The Squier firm was consulting for *Al Gore's* campaign. It may have been the first time in American political history where one consulting firm had a monopoly on all the candidates running in a party's presidential primaries. Why either campaign or anyone in the Democratic Party would think this is a good idea is beyond me. But I'm sure it was good for the Squier firm—a charter member of Election Industry, Inc.

As the somnolent Bradley campaign crept toward irrelevancy on quiet little cat feet, Al Gore, his consultants, and his campaign operatives made a hash out of his run for president. By fall 1999 the Gore campaign's ineptness had somehow managed to make the Democratic primaries competitive. The media and the Democratic Party insiders were questioning whether Gore had the leadership skills and enough Clintonesque affection of the voters to win the primaries, much less the general election.

Gore's answer was (in his mind) a bold move: He would relocate his campaign headquarters to Nashville! Gore explained himself on a late September *Today Show* appearance that I happened to catch in a Miami hotel room. When Al Gore launched into his smarmy, unctuous, and patronizing explanation to Katie Couric, I just shook my head. When he talked in those dulcet and overly sincere Southern tones—the same way one would address a slow, dumb child—about how this clearly calculated political move would reinvigorate and free up his campaign, I began to get agitated. But when he had the unmitigated gall to position himself as some sort of *Easy Rider* rebel by quoting Janis Joplin (actually, Kris Kristofferson)—"Katie, sometimes freedom's just another word for nothing left to lose"—I was screaming at the TV and looking around the room for something to throw at the screen: a remote, a Bible, a piece of artwork, anything. Fortunately, it was one of those hotel rooms in which everything is nailed down or screwed to the walls. Otherwise, it may have been the first instance of a politician quoting a rock star—and not the rock star himself—being responsible for the trashing of a hotel room.

I didn't realize it at the time, but what I was watching was a preview of how maladroitly Gore and his campaign would kick away the election thirteen months later.

Entering the 2000 election year, people were looking for a hero. They found John McCain.

McCain has done some terribly brave things in his life. One was spending a miserable number of years as a prisoner of war after being shot down, having both legs broken, and nearly drowning during the Vietnam War. Another was sponsoring and passing campaign finance reform, which took a lot longer than the time he spent in a Vietcong prison, and gets him treated in the Senate nearly as well.

So when John McCain, a Republican, agreed to work on what is traditionally a Democratic issue—campaign finance reform—and even to co-sponsor the legislation with Wisconsin Democrat Russ Feingold, you can imagine the fallout. It's one thing for a Democrat to get behind campaign finance reform. It's much harder for a Republican, especially a Republican of McCain's high profile.

Throughout 1999, Election Industry, Inc. spoke with one loud and self-serving voice. Whether Republican or Democrat, every pollster in America was advising all candidates in the two major political parties that campaign finance reform was a non-issue. They said over and over again that campaign finance didn't matter to voters, that taxes and crime and education (or, as I call them, the Usual Suspects) were far more important to voters in their daily lives. Of course, the polls were funded by the two major political parties, who were 100 percent against campaign reform, so—perhaps not surprisingly—their findings were *remarkably* consistent with the views of the people who were paying for them.

The pernicious influence of big money in politics has had a cancerous effect on the population for at least the past few election cycles, where big money has increased exponentially. If they pay any attention at all to political campaigns, voters who have grown up being told that everybody's vote counts the same soon realize that it doesn't. While a poor person's vote doesn't affect the end tally any less than a rich person's vote (assuming both actually get counted), the rich donor or fundraiser gets far greater access to the elected official they both might support. And organizations that form PACs—the chief source of "soft money" contributions to candidates and to the two major political parties—seem to get the laws they want, written the way they want, whenever their candidates get into office.

Against this backdrop, John McCain blithely kept talking about the non-issue of campaign finance reform, plugging away despite what the Election Industry, Inc. professionals were saying. He did so because it was the right thing to do. And the people noticed, and liked what they saw.

In the spring of 2000, McCain's campaign and his Straight Talk Express campaign bus were all that voters everywhere wanted to talk about. When I questioned some of these younger, more progressive voters—about how conservative McCain was on many social issues, or how important campaign finance reform really was to them—the voters indicated that only one thing really mattered: honesty.

After years of Clinton and Gingrich and partisan politics

and Monica and more Clinton, people wanted a public official that they could believe in—and just plain believe. It was the Paul Wellstone and Jesse Ventura case history all over again. When you are the one candidate who is perceived as being honest with people, you can accomplish amazing things. When you give the press nearly unfettered access to your campaign and to yourself—because you have nothing to hide—it should come as no surprise that the press will write something favorable. And when you underscore that honesty by taking away one of your own major election advantages as an incumbent, and tell people you are doing it because it is the right thing to do, you don't need a bunch of steatopygous pollsters from Election Industry, Inc. to tell you which way the political winds are blowing. You'll hear it every day from the people you meet.

Even so, honesty wasn't enough. Defeated by the advantages George W. Bush had in money and—largely due to his father—Republican insider contacts (as well as some low blows in the South Carolina primary), John McCain shut down his campaign after being badly beaten in the Super Tuesday primaries. It had been a hell of a ride on the Straight Talk Express, but Election Industry, Inc. had fingered their boy, and it wasn't John McCain. Ultimately, his campaign could not fight on so many fronts at once.

But there was still a battle going on. And this time he was the battleground.

In March of 2000, there were still some of us in the anti-Perot and anti-Buchanan factions of the Reform Party who held out hope that we could find a candidate who could advance the independent movement further. Once the Republican nomination was decided, we saw that our best hope might be Mr. Straight Talk himself: John McCain.

The political realities were there. McCain's campaign had done such a good job that in hypothetical three-way races—

Bush, Gore, and McCain—he was attracting between 25 percent and 35 percent of the vote. What's more, an independent McCain run for president had important advantages. He would be able to raise money, and lots of it. We had already projected that we could be very competitive with only $25 or $30 million over the rest of the campaign, even though Bush's and Gore's spending would each likely triple that amount. McCain could easily raise $50 million if he decided to take on Election Industry, Inc.

Just as importantly, we believed we could leverage an independent McCain for President campaign into the kind of movement that would immediately coalesce political independents, and bring out young people, first-time voters, and lapsed voters. And it would be very difficult to keep an independent McCain out of the presidential debates (though I'm positive the two parties would have tried to do so).

We tried to talk him into it. The key question was whether McCain, a lifetime Republican in a Republican state, would leave the GOP. The only historical precedent was Teddy Roosevelt, who left the Republican Party in 1912 and ran for president as the Bull Moose Party candidate. We had heard that McCain and his campaign staff were more than a little perturbed at the way Bush had won the primaries and the support he had received in doing so from the national GOP. We heard that he might be mad enough to quit the party. We put in our two cents worth of analysis and our projections, and let people know we were ready to go if McCain could be convinced.

The Republican establishment, which had ignored McCain since the primaries and dismissed the rumblings that he might do such a thing, quickly found out that there was a serious effort afoot to lure McCain away from the party. While McCain was out of the country on a well-earned postprimaries vacation, they sent out senior Republican colleagues of McCain's from the Senate to assure reporters that John

McCain wouldn't think of doing such a thing, that he was a loyal Republican, and that he would soon announce that he was backing George W. Bush for president.

Complicating McCain's decision was the way the Republicans were handling it. If they had done nothing, they probably would have been better off: the senator would have looked at the big picture, logically analyzed it, and come to the conclusion that there was nothing for him to do but to be a good soldier and take one for the team. Instead, the lobbying intensified, in the worst sort of Washington-insider way. Rather than talking directly to McCain, the Republicans were communicating their messages to him through the press.

One leading Republican after another would step forward to assure the press and the public that a "proud Republican" and "strong American" like John McCain would never, ever leave the Republican Party. Longtime friends and colleagues of McCain were pushed forward to talk about how the party had always stood behind him (not even close to true, especially on his campaign reform efforts) and how he would never wreak the kind of damage this could cause to his party and his political home for so many years.

No one from the Bush campaign would talk to McCain, either. They were taking a hard line: they won, he lost, he should be coming to prostrate himself before them, to seek reconciliation and to honor them with his tribute and his endorsement. They were jealous of the continuing national attention McCain was receiving, and perhaps a little embarrassed about their own conduct during the campaign. In fact, the Bush people probably didn't care if he left the party, figuring it would be suicidal for his career, and would eliminate a possible maverick contender to their reelection in 2004.

No doubt there were threats of retribution as well. Although he was not up for reelection until 2004, Republicans certainly were not shy about letting McCain know that he would be considered a pariah if he defected and attempted to stay in the Senate, and that any legislation he supported would suffer—as would his constituents—if he pursued such folly.

Of course, threats, avoidance, and circumlocutions are exactly the way to make a person like John McCain get his back up. So whatever calming effect his South Seas vacation had was probably lost within minutes of returning to Washington. And these threats and prevarications likely made him consider the possibility of an independent run for president far longer than he would have had Republicans remembered the name of his campaign transportation, and dealt with him in a straight-talking manner.

Eventually, he made good on his promise to endorse his party's nominee, though he turned out to be at best a reluctant campaigner for the man who defeated him. Today, McCain claims he never really considered an independent run for president, that it was flattering but impossible. But I believe it was a missed opportunity for him—candidates usually get only one chance when a favorable constellation of factors lines up like this. In his heart, I believe, there is some lingering regret that John McCain didn't continue his refreshing presidential quest and take a real shot at becoming our first independent president in over a century.

In March of 2000, after George W. Bush had finally eliminated John McCain, I let the Democrats know we were not that keen on working for Al Gore. But at the same time I started sending messages that we would definitely be interested in doing ads—in our own inimitable style—that would get people laughing about the notion of George W. Bush as President.

They weren't interested. After all, I wasn't one of them, and I certainly wasn't a party-approved member of Election Industry, Inc.

One of the multitude of mistakes the Democrats and the Gore campaign made was not taking out Bush early. Not doing so led to the eleventh-hour smear campaign regarding Bush's drunk driving arrest, which backfired on Gore's campaign when most people saw it for what it was—a calculated, last-minute, political dirty trick, typical of the desperate levels Election Industry, Inc. will sink to when an election hangs in the balance.

The time for the Democrats as a party to go after Bush was earlier in the year. You would think they learned nothing from Bill Clinton's surprisingly easy reelection in 1996. The main reason Clinton won so handily is that the Democrats defined Bob Dole and the Republicans before Dole even had a chance to get dressed as a presidential candidate. The Democratic Party was running ads nearly a year in advance of the election, ads that took Bob Dole—a war hero, longtime leader of the Senate, and by most accounts, a decent and witty man—and turned him into everyone's mean uncle. Clinton's team put Dole into a box he could never escape.

George W. Bush was far from a highly skilled national candidate himself. He had been held captive by his own advisers in Austin during the latter part of 1999, in a tutorial cram session to try to get him ready for prime time. Why? Because he was generally perceived by the public *not* to be ready for prime time.

The Democrats could have taken advantage of his weakness in early 2000, during the Republican primaries while John McCain was getting so much traction. Or immediately coming out of the primaries, when even many Republicans were questioning the Bush campaign's tactics in dispatching McCain, and while the general public was still unsure as to whether he was quality presidential material or not. Or even as late as early in the summer.

In a typically wonkish mistake, the Gore campaign did try

to attack some of Bush's proposals and policies in June. But George W.'s strengths were not in proposals and policies—they were totally contained in his personality as a likeable guy and a capable executive. Destroy either of those two perceptions, and Bush would have been charred meat on a Texas barbecue by late summer.

There was no need even to consider going near his past personal problems in order to get the country laughing at him. This was a man who couldn't find oil in Texas during a time when it seemed like all anybody else had to do was fall down and oil would spurt up. His company was forced into a distressed sale to avoid bankruptcy and triggered a Securities and Exchange Commission (SEC) investigation into whether he engaged in insider trading. And he was going to be the candidate of big business and the chief executive of the country?

After failing in the oil business, this is a man who used sweetheart loans from his daddy's friends—OPM, or "other people's money," as they say down in Texas—to install himself as a managing partner of major league baseball's Texas Rangers. There, he parlayed public subsidies for a new stadium into a deal that would ultimately enrich him to the tune of more than $15 million (on a $600,000 original investment). What else did he do as managing partner of a baseball team? Just trade Sammy Sosa, who would go on to become the first player in major league history to hit over sixty home runs in three consecutive seasons.

Since the Alamo, Texans have always taken pride in their ability to stand tall and fight. Here was one Texan refusing to take a stand on anything, and who wanted desperately to avoid any fights. We started to play around with notions such as portraying Bush as a blank check who would be filled in by his monied overseers once he got elected, or making fun of his avoidance of the issues by setting commercials to the tune of "Nowhere Man" or "The Wanderer" ("I'm the type of guy you could never pin down. . . .")

There was plenty more substantive grist for the mill, too, most of it stemming from the sad state of the state of Texas. Under George W. Bush as governor, Texas was ranked:

- 50th in spending for teacher's salaries
- 49th in spending to protect the environment
- 48th in per-capita funding for public health
- 47th in delivery of social services
- 42nd in child support collections
- 41st in per-capita spending on public education
- 5th in the percentage of residents living in poverty
- 1st in air and water pollution (Houston having recently passed Los Angeles as the major city with the worst air in America)
- 1st in the percentage of poor working parents without health insurance
- 1st in the percentage of children without health insurance
- 1st in death penalty executions by the state (a prisoner was executed on average once every two weeks during George W. Bush's five years in office)

You'd think even Al Gore's bumbling campaign would have been able to do at least a little with all that.

Nader 2000

A week before Election Day 2000, Ralph Nader and his campaign manager were wrapping up a discussion with me about our travel and media strategy when he asked the question we had no way of knowing we were a lot more than a week from answering: Who's going to win?

I had been noodling around with Electoral College vote calculations for the past few days, trying to identify states that were going to go overwhelmingly for Bush or for Gore in order to formulate a strategy whereby we might get some supporters for the obvious winner—or loser—to change their vote to Nader. "Not only can I tell you who's going to win, I can tell you why, and show you exactly on the map where the election will be decided," I said.

"It's all going to come down to Florida," I said, and walked confidently over to the map behind Ralph's desk. "Specifically, it's all going to come down to *here*," and I traced an area on the east coast of Florida from just north of Miami to just south of Vero Beach.

I'm not psychic, and it wasn't a parlor trick. We had worked for an independent U.S. Senate candidate in Florida earlier in the year, and had done our usual thorough targeting. We had divided the state into more than a dozen distinct areas, and this one, I explained, contained retirees and transplants, many of them Jewish, from New York and Philadelphia and New Jersey.

"And Al Gore will win Florida," I concluded, "because he selected Joe Lieberman as his running mate."

I had everything right. Except the (ultimate) winner.

According to my back-of-the-envelope projections, only three states were still in play—Florida, Missouri, and Michigan—with Wisconsin (if you pushed me) a possible fourth. I predicted that all but Missouri would go for Gore, bringing him the victory. I was wrong about Florida, obviously, and I didn't see Maine going to Gore or West Virginia and Tennessee going to Bush. And even though I was right about all the others, I was wrong enough to call the race for the wrong guy.

That's how small the battlefield for the last presidential election was. In their pursuit of Electoral College votes, the Gore and Bush campaigns narrowed the race down to only about a dozen states where the final outcome between the two looked like it might be in question. That's where both campaigns tended to do most of their work, while they virtually ignored the rest of the country. If you were in any one of the other thirty-eight states or the District of Columbia, in the infinite wisdom of Election Industry, Inc., you were pretty much bypassed by the two major-party presidential campaigns.

But there was an entirely different presidential race going on at the same time. While Bush and Gore were locked in a battle for a majority of electoral votes, Ralph Nader and Pat Buchanan were engaged in campaigns with a somewhat more democratic objective: they just wanted to get votes, as many as possible, anywhere, to maximize their popular vote total.

Each candidate needed to get 5 percent of the vote—about 5 million votes—for his respective Green or Reform Party to attain or keep major-party status (and claim the future public campaign financing money that comes with it). A vote in Idaho was every bit as good as a vote in New York City for Nader or Buchanan. Strategically, that meant that Nader and Buchanan had to go wherever they could to find votes. Ralph Nader actually campaigned in all fifty states—flying commercial (coach), on a senior citizens' discount, no less—trying to talk to *all* the people, not just those in the handful of "swing" states which Election Industry, Inc., deigned to anoint as "in play."

The Nader campaign was an entirely different animal than the more specialized efforts orchestrated by the major parties. And Election Industry, Inc. was more than happy to treat us as if we were in a completely different race whenever it suited its purposes, such as when it was time for national debates. But when it was time to find someone to blame for their many mistakes, we weren't ignored—we were subjected to the entire array of their standard bag of major party tricks.

Ralph's pledge to campaign in all fifty states was central to our agreeing to work with him when he contacted us in January. He had supposedly run in 1996, but he raised no money and basically campaigned from behind his desk. This time he was running for real; his supporters were already engaged in fundraising and petitioning to be on the ballot in all fifty states. Though the Nader 2000 campaign was going to be light on money, it would be deep in heart, commitment, and volunteers.

Frankly, the fifty-state pledge scared me. It seemed to indicate that Nader's effort would stretch countrywide and about an inch deep. I wanted a very disciplined approach: measurable, achievable campaign objectives that we could all agree on. We wanted some budget assurances and an understanding of how Ralph would campaign. We wanted to do some hard targeting studies and to consolidate the campaign's resources in areas where we stood to get the most return on our investment of money and manpower.

Nader's campaign manager, Theresa Amato, negotiated an agreement that went beyond a standard duties-and-dollars contract to stipulate strategic objectives and assumptions for the campaign. I'd never had a contract like this, with any client. But it showed me they were serious.

Our goal was to get at least 5 percent of the popular vote, thereby qualifying the Green Party for major party status in America. To do so, we would use voter targeting to identify the areas most likely to generate the greatest number of popular votes for Ralph Nader, and would focus our efforts on those areas. We would raise awareness among the general public about how Ralph's many accomplishments have positively affected the daily lives of most American families. We would position the campaign in a credible way to the press and thereby give it legitimacy, not allowing it to be marginalized either by the candidate's party affiliation or by his 1996 campaign. And we would force our way into the presidential debates, perhaps with Reform Party candidate Pat Buchanan in tow.

The candidate's credibility was obviously not an issue. Among the organizations Ralph Nader has founded and nurtured are Public Citizen, the Center for Auto Safety, and the Center for Women's Policy Studies; he also played major roles in creating the Environmental Protection Agency, the Freedom of Information Act, and OSHA. As a result, all of us in America today enjoy cleaner air and water; better and stronger consumer protection laws (which have led to better consumer products);

higher wages; safer working conditions; safer food products; expanded civil rights; better and safer automobiles; greater protection of individual privacy rights; and more information from and greater supervision over our government.

Even with Nader's credibility, I could see that establishing and maintaining the legitimacy of his candidacy would be our first assignment. The work of converting interest and acceptance into votes would come later, right around the time he was mopping the floor with the other candidates in the debates, if we were lucky. But heading into convention season, I was eager to sell the public on candidate Nader's legitimacy in the way I knew best, through advertising that would show the public and the press that a vote for Nader was a vote for something important and different, and not just a vote taken from Al Gore and given indirectly to George W. Bush.

There were a couple of hitches in this plan: Nader's campaign didn't have much money, and the candidate was loath to put what he did have in the hands of the TV networks to broadcast our commercials.

I never expected that we'd compete with the other candidates on the money front. I knew we wouldn't have the $150 million-plus of the two major-party candidates, or the $13 million that Pat Buchanan would get as the Reform Party candidate, or even the $5 to $7 million that Buchanan would raise on top of his public financing money. There was no way we were going to be able to come close to any of those figures.

We told the Nader campaign that they would likely need to spend a minimum of $3 million on media in order to get 5 percent of the vote; it would be pretty much impossible to compete nationally with anything less. But the campaign believed they would only be able to raise as much as $5 million total. After backing out costs for travel, campaign staff, field organization, campaign materials, overhead, and so on, it meant we would have to try to develop media plans at truly skimpy levels. Ultimately, we agreed to devise three plans: a $500,000 level, a $1.5 million level, and a $2 million level.

Even these low levels took a lot of convincing. Nader hates the consolidation that is taking place in the major media, where most of our "free" press is now controlled by a handful of large corporations. He especially hates the notion of a candidate's need to buy expensive television advertising time, essentially paying these big media conglomerates for the privilege of making his case to the American people.

I don't disagree with Ralph on this—in fact, we've worked hard with the Alliance for Better Campaigns to expose the insane costs for political airtime, information that ultimately led to an overwhelming Senate vote to close loopholes the TV stations were exploiting. Ralph is a big believer in grassroots fieldwork and radio advertising, so much so that I think he would have run his entire campaign's advertising on public radio stations if he could. But the indisputable reality remains that the most efficient and effective means of speaking to a lot of people in a short period of time is TV advertising.

Sometimes the right commercial delivers both a controlled message and a level of free media attention that outstrips what any ad budget could afford. Such was our good fortune with our first major TV commercial, launched in the weeks between the Republican and Democratic conventions, traditionally a time when neither major-party candidate is advertising heavily. As expected, we had the advertising stage virtually to ourselves. Even better, we generated the kind of press that could only be described as "priceless."

By this point we had been developing our advertising approach for months, and had decided that the notion of parodying already-successful ad campaigns made the most strategic sense. Doing so would underline the campaign's anti-corporate credo, and tying Nader's ads into campaigns that were already familiar would make them both funnier and a lot more effective on our very limited media budget.

Every high-profile ad campaign was fair game. For a debate message, we developed a parody of Budweiser's "Whassup?" ad campaign. We conjured up a great get-out-the-vote message that revolved around a parody of Nike's "Why I Run" commercials. We had print parodies of both Volkswagen's "Drivers Wanted" campaign and Apple's "Think Different" campaign. And then there were the few spots we actually, finally produced, beginning with our parody of MasterCard's campaign, a commercial we called "Priceless Truth."

One of the first times anybody saw "Priceless Truth" was on *Meet the Press*. Tim Russert had invited Nader, John McCain, and (by satellite from Minnesota) Jesse Ventura to be on the show that Sunday, August 6th. Russert had requested a copy of "Priceless Truth," and we all assumed he would use it during the interview with Ralph. Instead, he sprung it on John McCain, using it as an entrée into a discussion about campaign finance reform. He also put McCain on the spot, asking him what he thought of the ad. So the first national reviewer for "Priceless Truth" was Senator John McCain, who gave it a big thumbs-up.

"Priceless Truth" started to air that Sunday in about a dozen major markets around the United States. By the time the Democrats gathered in Los Angeles for their national convention a week later, people all over the country were talking about "Priceless Truth," as were the chattering classes in Washington. The press conference we had called in Washington the day after Ralph's *Meet the Press* appearance to introduce it had the media sitting up and taking notice of our campaign for what seemed to be the first time.

We had carefully parceled out our paltry media dollars to get as much national impact as we possibly could. And impact it had. In our stronghold markets, Nader's awareness and support shot up almost overnight. The buzz "Priceless Truth" was generating was unparalleled, and would dominate the presidential campaign ads until the Bush campaign's "Rats" controversy many weeks later. In fact, it was going so well we decided to extend the buy in California right through the Democratic National Convention, which drove the party's delegates nuts. (It also drove the people at MasterCard nuts; though political advertising is protected as free speech, MasterCard filed a lawsuit against the Nader campaign over the ad.)

"Priceless Truth," was a true hit. The *New York Times* said it broke the formula for political ads and called it the first truly irreverent candidate commercial of the election. Oddly, the reporter felt that the ad was hyperbolic in our listing of the amounts spent on fundraisers and ads and campaign promises; actually, we intentionally *underestimated* some of the amounts in the commercial, because the true value of "promises made to special interest groups" is, sadly, just too high to be believed.

"Priceless Truth" didn't single out either Democrats or Republicans as worse offenders, but Nader was particularly vocal in his own harsh judgments of Gore. Ralph believes in accountability, and he held Gore to a higher standard than Bush, especially once the Democrats started attacking Nader after their convention. He was incensed when Gore would outright lie or pander to people or when he would attempt to cover up some major and harmful deficiencies in the Clinton/Gore years. Ralph really did believe that Gore's record of incrementalism in Congress and as part of the Clinton administration was more harmful to many people than many policies of the Reagan years, and he didn't want Gore to get away with glossing over it.

While much has been made of Nader's statement that

there was no difference between Gore and Bush except for their rhetoric (in point of fact, they did agree thirty-seven times in their second debate), he was most assuredly not the only progressive who felt that way. As Studs Terkel said, "Choosing between Gore and Bush is like choosing between influenza and pneumonia." A few of us in the campaign put it a different way: "Bush and Gore make me wanna Ralph." And looking at Gore's record, there was plenty to make you, well . . . Ralph. In fact, you could pretty much pick your issue:

> **Al Gore, the noted *Earth in the Balance* environmentalist?** According to the League of Conservation Voters (who would cynically attack Ralph Nader later in the campaign), Gore's environmental voting record was below average for a Democrat in the House and Senate.

> **Al Gore, staunch defender of women's rights?** While in Congress, Gore consistently opposed federal funding of abortion for poor women, and voted with anti-choice forces nearly 85 percent of his time in Congress.

> **Gore/Lieberman, fighting the big drug companies and looking to lower your prescription drug prices?** Lieberman was the single biggest recipient in Congress of contributions from pharmaceutical and health insurance companies.

> **Al Gore, champion of civil rights?** In 1980, when the IRS looked to enforce equal opportunity laws by denying tax-exempt status to schools that did not admit black students, Gore aligned himself against the legislation.

Al Gore, friend of labor? In one of his earliest votes in Congress, Gore was one of a handful of Democrats whose swing votes helped defeat a bill that would expand labor's restricted rights to picket.

Al Gore, appointer of liberal Supreme Court justices? While in the Senate, Gore voted to confirm both Antonin Scalia and Clarence Thomas.

Al Gore, crusader against the dangers of smoking? Gore spent the seven years after his unctuous 1992 convention speech about his sister's death from lung cancer on Tobacco Road, mining campaign contributions from the tobacco industry, and even accepting government subsidies for tobacco allotments on his own land. His Election Industry, Inc. presidential campaign consultants were firmly in the pockets of Big Tobacco.

Who needs butterfly ballots to lose an election when you've got fluttering Al Gore as the candidate? Mixed messages like these would confuse anyone.

By late September, I was getting concerned about Nader's ability to get 5 percent of the popular vote. The wild card was the debates. If we could get Ralph on stage with King George II, Prince Albert, and Pitchfork Pat, we would have a spotlight, an audience and a platform for direct comparison that no advertising buy could accomplish. If we got into the debates, I was confident we'd recover from the Democrats' post-convention attacks—in fact, we could probably use the attacks to our advantage. If we didn't get into the debates, without a critical mass of dollars for advertising to shore up our support, we would be in big trouble down the stretch—especially if the

Democrats stepped up their attacks, which seemed almost inevitable, since Al Gore and his campaign were doing such a good job making sure the election stayed close.

If the two parties learned nothing else from Ross Perot's 1992 run, they grasped the importance of televised debates for third-party candidates, a lesson that was reiterated—loudly— by Jesse Ventura's debate victories in 1998. By and large, debates are a threat to Election Industry, Inc. and to major party candidates (especially incumbents). They don't like uncontrolled situations. And even when they try to control the format of debates as much as possible, anything can happen in a debate. So there is far too much at stake during debates for the two major parties and their candidates.

For challengers, independents, and alternative candidates, debates are essential. They are the only situations in modern-day campaigning when candidates like these are on an equal and even footing with the two major party candidates. But the major parties know this too, and they have demonstrated the extremes to which they'll go to ensure that no third-party candidates share the debate stage with their own nominees.

The 1992 debates that so benefited Perot were actually the last presidential debates sponsored by the League of Women Voters, a nonpartisan volunteer organization that has been part of the backbone of American democracy since time immemorial. After Perot's 19 percent showing, the two parties got together and decided: Never again. Democrats and Republicans don't mind using each other to continually ramp up the fundraising game, but like gangsters or drug dealers, they don't want anyone else cutting in on their lucrative turf. So they created something called the Commission on Presidential Debates that now runs all of the debates (underwritten by corporate sponsors, of course).

Do you get to vote for who sits on this commission and makes up the rules for the presidential debates? No, I'm sorry, you don't. The commission is made up entirely of Democrats and Republicans who are loyal to the party and who do what their party leadership tells them to do. That's why you didn't see Ross Perot in the 1996 presidential debates, and why I knew we wouldn't get Ralph Nader into the 2000 debates without a fight and without a huge public outcry.

I had told the Nader campaign since the very beginning that if we could participate in all three debates, there's no telling how high we could go. It was the ideal setting for people to get to know Ralph; a setting in which they could directly contrast him with the other candidates. I knew we would fare well in any such comparison, and I was willing to spend our limited ad money to try to make it happen.

The strategy of using ads to build public outrage to get Nader into the debates was a sound one, but it required more financial resources than the campaign had, especially in August and September. We needed to do a series of TV spots and to air them at higher levels than we could afford in order to reach enough people to put pressure on the two major parties and on the debate commission. Election Industry, Inc. was counting on their assumption that the press would not make a major issue out of candidates being excluded from the debates, and they were confident that the public would not pick up on it if no one other than the Naders and the Buchanans of the world were complaining. In short, they gambled, and gambled correctly, on press and public apathy.

The day we learned that Nader definitely would not be in the debates was the day I truly began to worry that we wouldn't hit 5 percent—at least not without a major advertising campaign in October, totaling at least $3 million. (Still, I don't think any of us could have envisioned how much damage Gore would self-inflict on his campaign by his performance in the debates.) Though most of the states had settled fairly clearly into one column or the other by late October,

Gore's debate performances left the last few key swing states far closer in the final weeks than either side expected. And when our electoral system gets reduced to a handful of swing states, odd things start to happen within the echo chamber in which Election Industry, Inc. exists.

You would think these supposed masters of manipulation would be too smart to be manipulated themselves. Hardly. Take for example the specious poll in late October that showed Gore's lead slipping down to 5–7 points over Bush in California. Suddenly the sky was falling! Gore's people panicked and fell for a bluff by the Bush campaign, which started talking about pouring some money into California for TV ads. The Gore campaign used this as another excuse for attacking Ralph, on whom it blamed its alleged California slippage. But in fact, the Gore campaign was thrown into a tizzy in California by the practitioners of Election Industry, Inc.—including Gore's own party.

How did it happen? The Democratic chairman in the state of California, Art Torres—like all state party chairs—has to raise money. California was safe for Gore, but the state and national Democrats had to scare people about the Nader threat in California because California is where the big money is for Democrats, and they needed it for other races besides Gore's— actually, for use practically anywhere *but* California. So the state and national Democrats start wringing their hands and saying, whoa, maybe it *is* getting close here—and they shake down their regular donors by saying, "George W. is closing the gap, and he may come in here with a big TV buy, so all you good Democrats in California have to get out your checkbooks again."

Then some reporter has to write about this nonsensical California poll and needs a corroborating quote. He calls a state Republican Party honcho whose own fundraising has been all but dead because everyone knows the state is going to Gore, so the main Republican fundraising draw—Bush—has treated California like it's quarantined. But the Republicans need to raise money. So, as earnestly as he can, this Republican honcho solemnly confesses that yes, we are getting pretty close, but we really don't want to tell anyone, otherwise the Gore campaign might notice.

Then the reporter calls Art Torres or some California party official like him, who knows the state is wrapped up but could use an excuse to raise more money for state and local candidates, and all of a sudden, BOOM! the echo chamber goes to work. One ill-informed beat reporter writes the story, other news outlets parrot it rather than looking like they got scooped, the pundits in Washington read about it and start huffing and puffing on the talk shows, the consultants hear and listen to the pundits, and like a self-fulfilling prophecy, the tipping point has been reached and the Gore campaign is suddenly hearing from everyone that *California is now in play!*

The Bush campaign puts a million dollar ad buy into California (which is beer money—spilled beer money, at that—for a campaign that will run hundreds of millions of dollars of advertising), and the Democrats and the Gore camp overreact, wasting some of their money and some of the candidate's time in California.

How did such an obviously wrong story get so much traction? Beyond the opportunism of both state parties, there might have been another, more insidious player in this scenario—the media itself. California TV stations were counting on a bonanza of presidential political advertising in 2000. When both campaigns got smart and decided not to waste their money in a state that was already decided, who was really taking it in the shorts? The stations. Which are owned by media conglomerates. Which also own . . . the very papers and television and radio stations where the polls and the stories about the polls were first reported. And where, of course, the extra national and state ad money raised by the controversy would be spent.

The reality was that Gore won California easily, just as he was going to all along—though later, in its craven scramble for excuses, his campaign blamed Nader for forcing them to spend time in California as a reason why he lost. But the canard worked to raise more money for both the Democrats and the Republicans. And, truth be told, it pulled a lot of support away from Nader. We were at 6 percent or more while the Gore campaign was being tricked, and we finished with only 4 percent of the vote in California. If people in California hadn't been panicked by this ridiculous poll into thinking the state was much closer than it was, Nader would have wound up with as much as 10 or 11 percent of the California vote.

A real presidential campaign speaks to all of the people in America, not just to key special interest groups in key swing states. A true presidential campaign needs an overarching theme and message—something every voter can understand about the candidate—not just a state-by-state series of tactics.

The only presidential campaigns that seemed to understand this were George W. Bush's . . . and Ralph Nader's.

If Nader was going to reach 5 percent of the popular vote, the last piece to the puzzle, I was convinced, was an ad in the final weeks that would give people a sense of empowerment, that would let them know that Nader's candidacy was about more than this election, and that would counter the "wasted-vote" argument that Gore and his surrogates (who included longtime liberal stalwarts like Gloria Steinem, Jesse Jackson, Paul Wellstone, and Massachusetts's gay congressman Barney Frank) were passing around like an infectious disease. The ad was "Grow Up," a parody of a Monster.com commercial that had struck a chord with people around the country when it aired on the Super Bowl a couple of years earlier.

Directed by the brilliant writer Scott Burns, "Grow Up" had kids mouthing sarcastic and cynical messages about what they expected from politics and politicians by the time they became adults. But the ad itself was anything but cynical, and it became the perfect counterpoint to the authentically cynical, inaccurate, and incessant attacks on Nader by the Gore campaign, by special interest groups tied to Gore, and by Gore's Democratic cronies and surrogates. "Grow Up" was a high road, high-minded call to arms for Nader supporters. It posed the most provocative question that can be asked in any national election: "What do you want from your government?" "Grow Up" would solidify our vote beginning in mid-October, and helped to undo some of the damage done by the Gore attacks.

In order to immunize people against the dread wasted-vote disease, however, we needed to have this ad up at least a couple of weeks before Election Day, where it would stand out positively against the other candidates' ads and where it could generate some talk value and momentum and word of mouth. But whether it was lack of money or lack of guts—or Ralph's famous antipathy towards all paid television advertising—the campaign didn't approve the ad until it was too late, in the very final days of the election.

The consequences of the delay were severe. By the time the ad got on the air, Nader had already been written off by the press and painted as a spoiler by the incessant attacks emanating from the Gore campaign and the Democrats. The dirty little secret about Nader's campaign, and the single biggest reason why we didn't reach our objective of 5 million votes, was that the campaign spent only $1.5 million on paid media advertising. And only $300,000 of that was spent in the general election period—the $300,000 worth of last-minute airtime bought for "Grow Up." It was far too little; far, far too late.

In the dwindling days of the election, as far as the press was concerned, we were yesterday's news. We were a good story in the second or third or even fourth week of October, but now everyone was fixated on the Electoral College race. I tried to tell Ralph that he was a nonfactor in electoral-vote swing states, where he would be ignored, and that it was preferable for us to go elsewhere and make the case to the people that we were in a popular vote race. Nader thought differently, believing that free press was the ticket, and he was willing to embrace the spoiler role if by appearing in swing states he would get the ink he craved.

I kept arguing for final days appearances in what we called "safe states" and on the West Coast. Ralph finally relented, but didn't want to travel cross-country again in the last three days. Instead, he agreed to a swing through New York, New Jersey, and Connecticut, all good states for our "safe vote" argument. But he also insisted on briefly visiting Florida, where we had never bought any media. On the Saturday before Election Day Ralph stopped in Miami for about an hour—not nearly enough to alter the outcome, and certainly no offset to Gore's VP candidate Joe Lieberman, who was down in Florida only about every four hours or so during the final weeks.

So if you want to believe Ralph Nader cost Al Gore Florida, and therefore the election, you'll have a hard time proving it. But if you really want to believe that, I have some evidence for you. It's been a secret so far. And it even had a mission code name—"Sunshine."

On the morning of October 16, five vans with teams of Nader volunteers, mostly college-age kids, departed from Washington, D.C. for long drives all over parts of the United States. Our strategy was simple. Since the two major-party candidates were focusing all their attention and their advertising on swing states in the final weeks of the election, why not send out a flotilla of volunteers into the many midsize media markets that were being overlooked by the two contenders? Our volunteers could organize impromptu demonstrations, perform a little street theater, distribute some campaign materials, then pack up and head on down the road to the next media market. At worst they'd be ignored, at best we'd be the lead presidential election story in town that day.

We supported the effort by developing a graphic design and look for the "Corporate Influence Clean-Up Crew," a logo that incorporated the "VoteNader.org" website address and that was plastered on the vans, on buttons, on soap wrappers (for the little bars of soap the crews would hand out), on mop buckets, and on spray bottles. The team of volunteers would pull up in the van, leap out in their Corporate Influence Clean-Up Crew coveralls and caps, and proceed to draw attention. Occasionally, volunteers would don rubber Bush and Gore masks, and stage two-party "debates."

The vans were scheduled to travel nearly 20,000 miles in three weeks. Vans and their routes had geographic code names: for instance, "Huck Finn" traveled up and down and around the Mississippi River; "Delta" spent most of its time in the Deep South. And then there was "Sunshine," whose route was to circumscribe the state of Florida. Starting out in Tampa on October 16th—the one van that did not emanate from D.C.—and returning to Tampa on Election Day, "Sunshine" logged nearly 2,000 miles, including stops in Fort Lauderdale and West Palm Beach.

As election night played out, it occurred to me that a few college kids in a van might have ultimately been responsible for the outcome. Consider: we spent no media money in Florida, and Ralph spent virtually no time in Florida, except for his few hours in Miami, where the "Sunshine" van itself never even made a stop. So, outside of any Green Party activity in the state (which was minimal—most Green Party rallies in Florida consisted of about one or two people) and the usual hotbeds of support surrounding college campuses, I am at a loss to explain the nearly 97,000 votes Nader got in Florida— except for the "Sunshine" van.

Of course, the "Sunshine" van, and the Nader candidacy, did not cost Al Gore the 2000 election, though I've heard many a moron claim otherwise. But if you happen to be one of those morons, consider this (taken from polling data, which morons seem to fetishize):

A CNN/Gallup tracking poll conducted just a couple of days before Election Day clearly exposed the miscalculation in the Gore campaign's claim that every vote not cast for Nader would come their way. As Richard Benedetto reported in *USA Today,* only 43 percent of the Nader supporters nationally said they would vote for Gore if Nader was not running, and another 21 percent said they would just stay home and not vote at all. Even if Gore lost by as little as one percentage point, Nader would have to get at least 5 percent of the overall popular vote to be a deciding factor; as it was, Nader got roughly half of that—only about 2.7 percent of the popular vote.

In other words, if Nader had not been in the race, Gore still wouldn't have gotten to 50 percent. Less than half of Nader's supporters would have voted for Gore—some would have voted for Bush, and a lot of them would have stayed home. (In Florida, Joe Lieberman notwithstanding, Bush got twelve times the number of *Democratic* votes that Nader did.)

I try never to attribute to malice that which is adequately explained by stupidity. But I'm having a hard time in the case of the Democrats who continue to dodge responsibility, to look for a place to point fingers, and to waste our valuable oxygen with their wailing and gnashing of teeth.

The lesson here has nothing to do with Nader and everything to do with Gore (and Bush): phony progressivism will lose to (slightly less) phony compassionate conservatism.

So did Ralph Nader's campaign accomplish anything?

I believe it did. Ralph's campaign clearly showed there are large numbers of people in this country who are still looking for more and better choices than the two major political parties are providing. If provoked, these people could become a compelling political force in the future, and with the continuing decline in political party identification, potentially a plurality.

Nader's campaign would have easily done better than 5 percent nationally if he had been permitted to participate in the debates, if he had spent more money on getting his message out, and if the Democrats had not taken it upon themselves to attack him personally and scurrilously over the final two months of the election. In fact, Nader would likely have reached 5 percent if any *one* of these things had taken place.

As it was, the campaign reached 5 percent or better in twelve states, firmly establishing the Green Party as the nation's leading third party and qualifying it for major party status (an important aspect for public financing) in many of those states. Ralph succeeded in mobilizing what he sees as a "watchdog" party, and its influence will be ongoing in states or districts where the progressive vote is an important part of the swing vote. As a candidate, Nader did not cave in and cut deals with the old, tired, and impotent Democratic Party, which is used to getting its way with liberals and progressives while delivering little but empty rhetoric to working people and minority voters over the past two or three decades. Nader reinvigorated young and old in a new breed of progressive politics that will not default to tired old Democratic liberalism.

Ralph's campaign raised nearly $8 million, a remarkable sum considering his very late start, the fact that he did not accept PAC money, and that nearly all of his contributions were from small donors: according to recorded donor lists, the average contribution was only about $170. And that does not include the thousands and thousands of people who made much smaller contributions when we passed the hat at Nader Super Rallies and at small gatherings.

Closest to my heart, Nader's candidacy brought at least a million voters who otherwise would have sat out the election back into participating in our democracy. Indeed, voter turnout in the 2000 presidential election was the highest ever, with more than a million more citizens casting ballots in 2000 than in the previous watershed year of 1992.

Not so coincidentally, 1992 had a major alternative candidate, Ross Perot, participating as well. Which begs the question as to how much higher voter turnout would have been had Nader—and even Pat Buchanan—been allowed into the presidential debates. Or if the American people were regularly presented with more choices than the two major parties and Election Industry, Inc. allow.

As I stayed up until 3:30 a.m. on that long and very odd November 2000 election night, Mike Wallace took to the airwaves of CBS and made an observation about the Nader campaign. He noted that candidates had spent as much as one billion dollars on television commercials during the election—"commercials that have assaulted and bored the dickens out of us the past few months." Wallace went on to say that there were just two ads that caught his fancy, and went on to show the nation, one more time, our "Priceless Truth" commercial, then concluded his commentary with our "Grow Up" commercial—a fitting exclamation point to an election bored to deadlock.

"They wouldn't let Ralph Nader into the debates," Wallace said. "He charged ten dollars for a seat at his crowded rallies.

He played it earnest and angry, mainly, in his speeches. And for millions of Americans, he managed to raise the questions and the doubts and to underline the disillusion that lots of us feel about how we wage our political campaigns."

Whatever Ralph's next move, Election Industry, Inc. better hang onto its hat. His supporters may have "Grown Up" a little since the 2000 debacle, and maybe we're now old enough to know better.

But we're still too young to give up.

Tale of the Tape

2000 Presidential Election: Popular Vote

Al Gore, Jr. (Democrat)	48%	(50,992,335 votes)
George W. Bush (Republican)	48%	(50,455,156 votes)
Ralph Nader (Green)	3%	(2,882,897 votes)
Pat Buchanan (Reform)	0%	(448,892 votes)
Harry Browne (Libertarian)	0%	(384,429 votes)
Howard Phillips (Constitution)	0%	(98,020 votes)
John Hagelin (Natural Law/Reform)	0%	(83,555 votes)

Third Parties in America

Sometimes people in America forget that we are a young country, a country that's not afraid to tinker with and change things when we find something that works better. There's nothing in our Constitution (and—I hope—in our constitutions) that says we all have to be Republicans or Democrats.

Like most Americans, I've always been intrigued by new ideas and new voices. Although I was too young to vote in 1968, the Democratic National Convention that year took place in my home town of Chicago, and the first political hero to capture my imagination was Minnesota Senator Eugene McCarthy. Running on an antiwar platform, "Clean Gene" took on the Election Industry, Inc. candidate (and his fellow senator from Minnesota) Hubert H. Humphrey. As I watched along with the rest of the world, the fracas outside on the streets of Chicago became a seminal event for political awareness among young people and for the peace movement. Soon, a whole counterculture was springing up, right outside my door.

But it seemed like the good guys never won. The bad guys never got caught or went to jail. The establishment always seemed to prevail.

So by 1972, I was tremendously excited. I was positive George McGovern was going to win! Everybody I knew was voting for him.

In the final days of the 1972 election, I went back to Chicago, where my two best friends, Rocky Chrastil and Roy Ginsburg, were serving as election judges. Hanging around the polls in Chicago—probably the most dependably Democratic city in the country—everyone we talked to was voting for McGovern. There was no doubt about it: in a stunning upset, George McGovern was going to ride the support of antiwar youth and peace-loving people all over America into the White House! It would be the ultimate middle-finger salute to the 1968 Democratic convention and the proof that my hero Gene McCarthy had been right all along.

Well, McGovern ended up getting only 37 percent of the vote and losing by 23 points. Hell, *Hubert Humphrey* had done far better than that, losing by less than 1 percent.

McGovern's defeat was a disillusioning but valuable lesson. In 1976, I became intrigued by Jerry Brown's ideas, but ultimately I settled for Jimmy Carter. Carter was an underdog and a populist and certainly more interesting than Gerald Ford, but he was no Gene McCarthy. Compared to McCarthy and Bobby Kennedy and George McGovern, Carter's politics seemed decidedly unexciting and middle-of-the-road.

Four years later, I cast my first vote for a true alternative to the two-party system, Independent candidate and former Republican congressman John Anderson. I knew Anderson didn't have much of a chance to win, but I liked him much better than the choice the two major parties had given me: Ronald Reagan or Jimmy Carter. And in voting for John Anderson, I learned another valuable lesson:

It's OK to vote for an independent or third-party candidate. You can do it. Nobody burst into the polling booth to ask me what I was doing. The ground did not open and swallow me up. Nobody followed me home.

You should try it sometime. You might even like it.

As everyone knows, Ralph Nader didn't hit the magical 5 percent mark in the popular vote of 2000. Five percent nationally would have established the Green Party as a major party in America. But with the success of the Nader campaign and the implosion of the Reform Party under Pat Buchanan, the Green Party is now the dominant third party in America.

Many people blame Nader and *those damn Greens* for costing Al Gore the election. They are wrong—Al Gore and his insipid campaign did a fine job of losing the election on their own. But if we had in fact swayed the results one way or the other, it would have been just the latest in a long line of presidential elections shaped by a third-party candidate, a tradition as rooted in our nation's history as the two-party system itself, and as recent as independent candidate Ross Perot delivering the presidency to the Democrats and Bill Clinton in 1992.

The two dominant political parties today don't like to bring this up, but there was a time when you didn't have to go through any party structure or litmus test in order to run competitively for public office. In fact, political parties didn't even exist until the presidential election of 1792. Before that election, candidates differentiated themselves simply by saying what state they were from.

In the very first presidential election by popular vote, four very qualified candidates from the same party all ran and split the vote. John Quincy Adams, Andrew Jackson (who lost—

despite winning the popular vote—when the election went to the House of Representatives), William Crawford, and Henry Clay were all members of the Democratic-Republican Party. That's right—the two major parties today were once joined at the hip and pretty much the only game in town back in 1824.

The dominant two-party system we have today got its start by accident. It took one of the most horrendous events in this country's history—the Civil War—to establish the Republican and Democratic parties. Immediately prior to Lincoln's election in 1860, the dominant parties were the Democrats and the Whigs. Martin Van Buren got over 10 percent of the vote as a member of the Free Soil Party in 1848 (helping to deliver the election to Zachary Taylor), and in 1856—the election immediately before Lincoln's—Millard Fillmore ran as the American Party candidate and took over 21 percent of the vote, giving James Buchanan the victory. (I wonder if the loser in that election groused that Millard Fillmore and *those damn Americans* cost him the presidency?)

When Abraham Lincoln ran for president in 1860, the Republicans were a third party in an increasingly fractured union. Stephen Douglas, the Democrat, would have defeated Lincoln easily if southerners had not splintered off into the Southern Democrat Party and taken 18 percent of the vote that year. *(Those damn Southern Democrats!)* And the Constitutional Union Party, another affiliation addressing the rancor of the time, ran a candidate who took nearly 13 percent of the vote. Lincoln won with less than 40 percent of the popular vote, to 30 percent for Douglas.

As the country went through a divisive war, the stability of just two parties looked like a good thing. So the elections of 1864 and 1868 were the first time a Republican campaigned exclusively against a Democrat.

Alternative or third parties have a long, colorful and important history in America. Traditionally, they have been a way to get other viewpoints on the table and into the national debate. Through all of our presidential elections, America's alternate or third parties have included:

- The Anti-Masonic Party (don't laugh—they got nearly 8% of the vote in 1832!)
- The National Republican Party
- The Whig Party
- The Liberty Party
- The Free Soil Party
- The American Party
- The Southern Democratic Party
- The Constitutional Union Party
- The Straight-Out Democrat Party
- The Greenback Party (over 3% of the vote in 1880, where the difference between the Republican and the Democrat candidates was .02%. *Those damn Greenbacks!*)
- The Prohibition Party (In 1884, the Greenbacks took about 1.75% of the vote and the Prohibitionists took nearly 1.5% of the vote— not much, but winning margins in a race where the Republican got 48.5% of the vote and the Democrat 48.25% of the vote. *Those damn Prohibitionists!*)
- The National Democratic Party
- The Union Labor Party (In 1888, the Prohibition Party got over 2% of the vote and the Union Labor Party a mere 1.3% of the vote. But the Democrat, Grover Cleveland, won the popular vote with 48.62% and still lost in the Electoral College to Republican William Henry Harrison, who had 47.82% of the vote. *Those damn Union Laborists!*)

- The Populist Party (8.5% of the vote in 1892, a race that the Democrat won by only 3% over the Republican. *Those damn Populists!*)
- The Bull Moose Party
- The Socialist Party (never much of a player, but around for a long time, from 1900 to 1940)
- The Farmer Labor Party (Minnesota's Democratic Party to this day is called the Minnesota Democratic Farmer Labor Party, or the DFL Party)
- The Progressive Party (nearly 17% of the vote in 1924, with candidate "Fightin' Bob" LaFollette from Wisconsin)
- The Union Party
- The States Rights Party
- The American Independence Party (nearly 14% of the vote went to their candidate, Alabama Governor George Wallace, a white supremacist, in an election Hubert Humphrey lost to Richard Nixon by .7%. *Those damn racists!*)
- The Libertarian Party
- The National Union Party
- The Reform Party (Ross Perot got 19% of the vote in 1992 as an Independent, 8% in 1996 as a Reform Party member. *That damn Perot!*)
- The Green Party (3% in 2000)

Those damn Greens!

The Internet and Politics

The internet is a remarkable communications tool for politics and political campaigns. But few campaigns understand how to use it, and very, very few have been able to realize its full potential.

One of those very, very few was Jesse Ventura's.

As the 1998 Minnesota gubernatorial election careered into its final weekend, the limitations of running an operation with so little money began to show through the highly buffed shine we had brought to the campaign. We were about to embark on our statewide seventy-two-hour Drive to Victory, a make-or-break strategy that was either going to show Minnesota a kind of bandwagon momentum it had never before seen, or have us limping and crawling to the finish line.

The strategy was high-risk, because the Ventura campaign did not have a lot of paid Election Industry, Inc. political operatives to advance the event, to build crowds, and to stoke the media machinery. We didn't have a strong, seasoned field organization or a statewide political party machine to tap into at each stop along the way.

What we *did* have was a new secret political weapon, one that flew below the radar of the other campaigns.

We had the best website.

In 1998, for most candidates, having a website was akin to scanning some campaign literature and making it appear on a computer screen. Few in politics understood what a powerful tool it could be. As a result, most websites were poorly designed, difficult to navigate, and hard to read. They took advantage of none of the interactivity or one-to-one communications ability that the internet offers.

Ventura's site was different. Throughout the election, the website had served as the repository for carefully reasoned and clearly written position papers containing Ventura's views on the issues. With news cycles getting shorter and quicker, and inaccurate or sensationalistic reporting becoming more common, our website saved us more than once. Whenever our candidate might make a particularly controversial remark, we were able to direct reporters and voters to the website, to get a "fuller understanding" or a "more balanced view" of Ventura's position. (Always remember: your supporters, your opponents—and sometimes the press—will all visit your website far more often than undecided voters looking for information.)

I was slackjawed at the amount of content on our website versus those of Jesse's competitors. Our website went up early—Coleman and Humphrey's sites took weeks to be ready, and their content was rudimentary at best. Most importantly, ours *worked*—it was functional and easy to navigate. (In the final days of the campaign, both Coleman's and Humphrey's websites went down with technical problems for many hours.

At one point very late in the campaign, we couldn't get past the home page on one of their sites for two entire days!)

But best of all, our website, like our candidate, was irreverent enough to be interesting. There was always something new happening on the Ventura website, which made it like catnip for his supporters. After we held a press conference to introduce the "Action Figure" TV commercial, one of the campaign's volunteer photographers borrowed the props and shot a number of digital photos of the Jesse Action Figure beating up on "Evil Special Interest Man." They were up on the website—and being downloaded—within a few hours.

The website also extended the reach of our remarkable TV spots. Because we received our public financing dollars so late in the campaign—the third week of October—all of our television spots appeared in a very condensed time frame. The ads were creating all sorts of interest and talk value, but because we had a very limited media budget, people did not see our ads nearly as often as Coleman's ads or Humphrey's.

So we put them on the website. Now whoever wanted to watch the ads could see them whenever they wanted to. But they had to come to our site to do it (this was before video files could be compressed enough to make it easy for people to email TV commercials to their friends—a strategy we pioneered in the next election cycle, with Ralph Nader's commercials). And once they arrived at the site, they found all sorts of other useful information about the candidate, his background, and his position on the issues. We used our TV spots like a beacon in the sky, drawing people to the destination of our website. And once they were there, we had 'em, and we could tell them anything we wanted them to know.

As the Drive to Victory moved through the state, everywhere we arrived, we were met by large, screaming, enthusiastic crowds. When we pulled into a small town in western Minnesota, hours behind schedule, and late on a Sunday night, no less, I was dumbfounded by the reception. "Where did all these people come from?" I asked. Not even the wiliest of Election Industry, Inc. advance teams would have been able to keep a crowd like this hours past its scheduled arrival time.

"The website," I was told. In much the same way you might call the airport to find out if your flight is delayed before leaving the house, we were updating our website hourly on the progress of the Drive to Victory, so people knew if we were running a little—or in this case, a *lot*—behind schedule.

Throughout the Drive to Victory, the website kept people all over the state informed every step of the way. But that's not all it did. The website made it personal for the voters. Not willing to rely only on the press we might get, we had arranged for volunteer digital photographers to rotate on to the route and then back to headquarters in the Twin Cities. There they would immediately post photos of the tour on a constantly updating basis.

And people could download the photographs from the website. So if you posed for a photo with Jesse on your Harley Davidson in the southern Minnesota town of Albert Lea at 11:00 on a Sunday morning, by midafternoon that same day the photo would be posted on Ventura's website, and you could download it and show it to your friends at dinner.

That's why Jesse Ventura's website is universally credited by political observers as the first effective use of the internet in politics, and why the American Association of Political Consultants designated it one of the very first websites to change the world of the internet and politics.

By the 2000 election cycle, you would think Election Industry, Inc. would have picked up on the potential of the internet.

You would think that, but you would be wrong.

The Internet and Politics

Neither Bush nor Al Gore—the self-ballyhooed Inventor of the Internet—did anything interesting with the web in 2000, besides waste a lot of money on it. Perhaps they were aware of their limitations. Not one time during any of their three nationally televised debates did either one of them mention his website or attempt to drive people to it.

Once again, the most interesting uses of the internet were to be found in the renegade campaigns, most notably the insurgent campaigns of John McCain and Ralph Nader.

McCain parlayed his reporter-loving media transparency and his "Straight Talk Express" image into booster-rocket momentum, especially among young people and political independents. Even more remarkably, McCain's was the first campaign to show definitively that the web was an important fundraising tool as well as a communications portal. He raised millions of dollars via his website in just a few weeks' time. In so doing, he single-handedly has guaranteed that the Washington bumblers and mishandlers will now turn their attention to the internet as a major new political tool, because nothing gets the attention of Election Industry, Inc. like a few million dollars in campaign contributions.

In our next major campaign after Ventura's—Ralph Nader's—the Nader website focused on that other important aspect of politics: votes. Ralph's website, woven mostly by a few young volunteer savants, was full of content and rich with media—everything from detailed position papers to detailed press releases to detailed policy proposals could be discovered, along with more entertaining fare, such as his convention video and our TV and radio ads. Nader's Super Rallies became a main focus of the website, building momentum by informing citizens all over the country about the crowds of 8,000 here, 10,000 there (15,000 at Madison Square Garden!), venues packed by people with questions that neither of the main party candidates had answers for.

213

Ralph's web strategy had a strong outreach presence as well, using email to contact and alert and organize supporters, a virtual field presence somewhat similar to that of Ventura's. Campaign materials were downloadable and desktop-publishable. With the advances in hardware and software, our ads became portable—downloaded, compressed, and emailed around the country from supporter to supporter. (With so little of the campaign's money ultimately going into paid media, there were times I felt that more people saw our ad messages over their computers than on their TV sets.)

Even Ralph's campaign was almost embarrassingly adept at raising money online. The campaign originally projected a $5 million operating budget, but ended up raising over $8 million, with much of that incremental money coming via web contributions.

By far the most interesting internet aspect of Nader's campaign was focused solely on votes—NaderTrader.com and related vote-swapping sites that showed up late in the election. As media speculation mounted on Nader's spoiler status, enterprising web-savvy supporters began an online campaign in which voters in safe states (states where Gore would win easily) would cast their vote for Nader. In return, a Nader supporter in a competitive Bush-Gore state would pledge to cast their vote for Gore.

The concept raised a hue and cry among the press, not to mention some ire from conservatives and Bush supporters, but it never really amounted to much more than blue-sky wishful thinking (after all, it was all on the "honor" system—there was no way to verify that either party would actually follow through on their agreement). But as electronic communications become ever more prevalent, speedier, and easier to use, some variation of this (especially in states which have not finished voting by the time early returns are reported) is sure to be employed.

So what's next for the Net in politics?

More web-based communications. The long-awaited McCain-Feingold campaign finance reform bill has a curious loophole—it does not address internet-based communications. For Election Industry, Inc., this may become the tipping point that moves campaign dollars away from tremendously wasteful television spending and on to the Web. What Washington really loves is raising and spending money, and money in politics, like water in a flood, has to go somewhere. If McCain-Feingold puts severe enough restrictions on political advertising in broadcast media, those dollars will find some other ways to be spent. And if campaign activities associated with the internet are largely exempted from McCain-Feingold, then you can bet your next political contribution is going to end up being wasted on the Web instead of annoying you on TV.

More outside group involvement. Attacks are nothing new in politics. But more and more, the attacks are coming over the internet. Commencing with each election cycle, there is now a race to stake out and sign up the rights to the most pejorative (and the most positive) web address names featuring the name of a candidate. Surprisingly, the creators of these besmirching names are often in the employ of the candidates being besmirched. Attackees want to get the rights to the names before the attackers can grab them and use them against their opponents. Entire websites are now constructed around names grabbed during these cyber-squatting contests, and some of them can be pretty effective at making fun of or attacking mainstream candidates. The biggest problem, as it is for anything web-based, is getting potential voters to visit the sites. But as cyberattacks and cyberbuffoonery become more common, you will see these independent attack sites become more skilled in doing web-based outreach to interest the curious in visiting their sites. (Much as one of the anti–George Bush sites did in 2000, luring net denizens to a site that compared George W. to the monkey, Curious George.)

"Wired workers" and "office park dads." These may become the "soccer moms" of the 2004 presidential campaign—an undeniable swing vote that may be able to be reached best via the internet. "Wired workers" are younger jobholders, often politically independent, whose occupation has them on a computer most of the day. They are extremely comfortable and facile with the web, and rather than getting away from a computer when they're off the job, they will often go right back online once they get home. They are computer savvy, know nearly all the best sites on the internet, and use it not just for work, but for information and entertainment. If a swing voter like this is constantly on a computer, how else are you going to reach them if not online?

"Office park dads" are similar in that they are generally employed by small businesses, information businesses, or in the high tech field, and nearly always found in a suburban location. While not as young or as net savvy as the "wired worker" group, office park dads do spend a significant amount of time on or around computers, and use it for a variety of purposes besides work (sometimes even while at work). Because they are both male and suburban, this swing vote bodes well for Republican candidates smart enough to figure out ways to get to them via the internet or via their computer.

Revenge of the print media. Everybody in Election Industry, Inc. seems to hate newspapers. They are convinced nobody reads them, that everybody watches television, and if people aren't watching television, they must be (briefly) listening to the radio. Consequently, members of Election Industry, Inc. would rather throw money down a rathole (or into direct mail—often the same thing) than put an ad in the newspaper, even on Election Day.

I've never understood this. The print media, and especially newspapers, drive the news coverage in nearly every market. TV uses the newspapers to tell it what's important to cover and also to develop story ideas for features or "newsmagazine" shows on the tube. In today's highly consolidated radio market, if a radio station even pretends to do the news anymore, it is little more than the deejay reading the morning paper aloud.

But newspapers and other print media, much more so than the "electronic" TV and radio media, have become the best adapters and developers of content and news sites on the web. Most newspapers now treat their websites as a twenty-four-hour edition of the newspaper—rather than just a morning paper, or a morning and an afternoon paper, we now have the latest news over the internet in a print-friendly format, whenever we need it.

Ironically, the print-based news sites are also becoming the leaders in using video and pushing the boundaries of effective advertising on the web. Banner ads and pop-up ads don't work—we all know that by now. Like traditional political advertising, all they seem to do is annoy people (which is probably why Election Industry, Inc. will embrace them wholeheartedly). But imagine what a streaming video ad in close proximity to relevant editorial content could do. Suppose your candidate, the incumbent governor, is being attacked in an article in the state's largest newspaper. A net-savvy political consultant could immediately film a "response ad," place it alongside the editorial on the paper's website, and have the window automatically open and the video run any time a reader clicked on the link to that particular story. Whether the ad departments are smart enough to sell online advertising this way—and whether the editorial people at the paper would allow it—is an interesting dilemma. But the technology is here, and I would think it's only a matter of time before ad-supported sites look to innovative ideas like this, and only a (slightly longer) period of time before campaigns and their consultants realize what a powerful tool this could become.

More creativity, especially in outreach. If a site is on the web but nobody goes to see it, does it really exist? That's not so much a philosophical question as an everyday truism.

There are interesting things happening all over the internet. Yet, much like the way Election Industry, Inc. does television ads, most political websites are crushing bores, sitting toadlike on the Information Highway. Other media must drive people to the website—not merely by showing the web address onscreen at the end of a commercial, but by truly integrating a campaign's website into the rest of its communications program.

At present, nearly all political websites do a truly lousy job at outreach. Where there was an excuse before—who wants to receive more email spam?—rich media like video, animation, illustration, games, interactive quizzes, and the like can all be easily sent and received electronically. Will this antagonize people? Only if it's not interesting. Like everything else in political communications, websites and web-based messaging cry out for greater creativity.

The ultimate political website. Website design companies tend to come in only two varieties—those skilled in graphic design, who make dynamic and interesting-looking websites filled with splash pages, Flash animation, and other eye candy, but which lack logic, navigability, and reliability. Or those skilled on the back end, who understand site architecture and navigability, with built-in redundancies for reliability, impenetrable firewalls, and whiz-bang programming and tech abilities, but who couldn't design something interesting or attractive if their code depended on it.

Like everything else they touch, the Beltway Bandits of Election Industry, Inc. charge way more than they deliver when it comes to putting together effective and interesting websites. The world cries out for someone to bring together the best practices of the web, in one integrated, affordable, customizable website, not just for political campaigns and organizations, but for independent groups and associations and nonprofits, all of whom have more similarities than differences.

If you build it, they will buy it.

Somebody needs to build it. Maybe it will be me.

Money in Politics
and How to Overcome It

The Washington-based political consulting industry and both major parties are constantly engaged in the collective work of convincing candidates and campaign managers that the road to victory was, is, and ever shall be paved with money—that whoever raises and spends the most money, especially on TV ads, inevitably wins.

The system as it is set up today benefits the political consulting industry (pollsters, spin doctors, media consultants, and the like) and the two major political parties who, via their national committees and senatorial and congressional campaign committees, play Daddy Warbucks for candidates who toe the party line.

Nearly every candidate I've talked to—including incumbents, who have a built-in advantage with the way the system is set up—hates raising money. They absolutely despise putting the arm on friends and supporters to max out at thousands of dollars a head, and they don't like feeling indebted to the businesses and special interest groups whose political action committees contribute money to their campaigns in a fairly transparent *quid pro quo*.

Voters aren't exactly thrilled with what comes out of this system, either. We are subjected to an incessant barrage of some of the most imbecilic advertising done anywhere in the world, advertising that the local TV and radio stations have no authority to remove (no matter how much it alienates their viewers or listeners) and for which federal candidates get a "sweetheart deal"—by law, they pay the lowest rates available.

Moreover, the way the system is set up, very few citizens can even consider running for office. In fact, during the 1996 election cycle, the Democratic Senatorial Campaign Committee (DSCC) was actively recruiting millionaires in many states to run against Republican incumbents, because the party was broke and only millionaires would have the necessary head start to raise enough money to compete.

So if candidates hate the system and voters hate the system, how is it possibly benefiting the country?

Despite the pervasive and pernicious dominance of big money in our elections, take it from me: there are ways to beat it. Political upsets like those of Paul Wellstone and Jesse Ventura are legendary mostly because they had to overcome such outlandish and incredible spending disadvantages.

Our approach to elections, as it turns out, is remarkably cost-effective. Paul Wellstone was elected senator in 1990 on a $400,000 media budget—less than one-tenth of what his opponent spent. Jesse Ventura was elected while spending only about $380,000 for media. Each of his opponents outspent him about six to one. Add in the soft money independent expenditures on their behalf, and Ventura's opponents outspent him by approximately $12 to 13 million.

We achieve dramatic results by outsmarting the competition rather than outspending them, and by doing innovative, creative communications that catch the audience's attention the first time they see them and that they look forward to seeing again.

Here's how we do it.

Be Honest with the Voters and the Press

One of the things that makes me fairly unique, in both politics and commercial advertising, is that I firmly believe in truth in advertising.

Whether for a branded product or a candidate, if you knowingly mislead your customers or the voters in your advertising, it is an abrogation of trust. If they have bought your product or voted for your candidate—or even if they are merely considering doing so—once you lie to them, you've lost them.

Political ads, if they are for a candidate running for federal office, cannot be censored. Unlike commercial advertising, you can say pretty much anything you want in a political ad and get away with it, and most campaigns and consultants take full advantage of this.

What I've never been able to understand about professional politicians and Washington consultants and all of Election Industry, Inc. is their inability to grasp the notion that a candidate's position on any given issue is meaningless unless the voters believe he is telling the truth.

Simple concepts like this are at the very heart of political upsets.

When most politicians open their mouths to speak, people have a preconceived notion that they are prevaricating. Most candidates for public office start at what I call a "minus twenty" on the truth meter. Both the press and the public have been conditioned through the years to believe that if a politician is campaigning and his lips are moving, he's lying.

When the press and the public believe that your candidate and your campaign are telling the truth, it is literally worth money in the bank. All the money that candidates have to spend to demonstrate their veracity—just to get to zero on the truth meter—is money you don't have to spend if people believe you are being straight with them.

I feel so strongly about this that at North Woods Advertising, we apply a much more stringent *commercial* standard of proof to all of our political ads. In fact, we have a clause in our contract that allows us to refuse to make any claim in our advertising that we don't believe we have sufficient proof for. Over the years, our political advertising has received uniformly positive reviews for accuracy (not to mention creativity) in the various ad reviews and ad watches conducted by the press. We've never had a negative review.

Taking the high road is the best way to reach your ultimate destination. In his first U.S. Senate campaign, Paul Wellstone captured the moral high ground and was seen by the public as a person of integrity—a committed, ethical candidate (if perhaps a little overly idealistic). Jesse Ventura was known as someone who would tell you the truth whether you wanted to hear it or not. Voters believed that both Wellstone and Ventura had nothing to lose by telling the truth—and consequently, they *didn't* lose.

Ross Perot got a great deal of early traction with the voters because he was perceived as someone who would tell them the truth, since he wasn't in league with special interest groups or in thrall to one of the two major political parties. John Mc-

Cain decried the influence of big money while giving the press virtually total access to himself and his campaign, most of it while riding in a bus called the "Straight Talk Express." Ralph Nader's presidential campaign drew on the good will established from nearly forty years of being a model of probity and being a consumerist—someone on the side of the people in their battles with big corporations, big bureaucracies, big government, and politicians too big for their britches. He has been called "the most honest man in America," and his book about his campaign, *Crashing the Party*, is aptly subtitled *How to Tell the Truth and Still Run for President.*

A candidate's personal credibility has a halo effect that goes beyond speeches and debates and rubs off on the campaign's other activities, like news releases and communications. It's a sad commentary on the current state of our politics, but because telling the truth is so unusual (and apparently so unexpected of candidates from the two major political parties), it is a tremendous motivator. Among the many things Jesse Ventura's election proved is this: when people believe that a candidate has nothing to lose by telling them the truth, that by itself has the power to engage the 40 or 50 or 60 percent of the population who have given up on the two major political parties and on participating in the process.

In politics, if your word is golden, it will help you compete against opponents with a lot more gold.

Forget Polling—Concentrate on Targeting

Until candidates, campaign managers, and political parties end their love affairs with the pollsters of Election Industry, Inc., inestimable amounts of money will continue to be wasted on elections. Accurate targeting enables a campaign to be immeasurably more cost efficient, in everything from media and mail expenditures to use of the candidate's time to the best way to deploy volunteers and field organization resources.

Most candidates and campaign managers are stupifyingly risk-averse. So they prefer to be told what to do by party-approved pollsters, whose data is presented to them as the best approximation of a "sure thing" that modern politics has to offer. Of course this is total nonsense, but candidates and campaign managers are rarely knowledgeable enough about communications or research methods or the "science" of polling to begin to ask the right questions, much less question the pollsters' answers. And because the best targeters are often people who are . . . well, pushing the boundaries of normalcy; and because targeting is as much the art of making educated assumptions as a science, candidates and campaign managers have a hard time understanding how targeting works (even though it is a relatively simple concept). So they are more comfortable with the false confidence, blandishments, and assurances of Election Industry, Inc. pollsters.

☆ ☆ ☆
Be Creative

Today's major party political campaigns have little imagination and even less creativity. Campaigns run by the major parties and their Election Industry, Inc. cronies are formulaic and predictable. The same averseness to risk of candidates and campaign managers that allows pollsters to take control of campaigns extends to the messages and the communications of the campaign as well. If we have done nothing else over the past decade, our work at North Woods Advertising has shown time and time again the true value of doing something unique and original in political communications. Commercials or communications that fail to interest or involve the audience are huge money-wasters for campaigns, and huge time wasters as far as the voters and the press are concerned.

That's why there are only three things posted on the wall of North Woods Advertising's conference room: a copy of the Declaration of Independence, a copy of the United States Constitution, and a sign that reads, "The only safe thing is to take a chance." If you are going to pull off a huge political upset at a great spending disadvantage, you aren't going to do it playing on the same turf and by the same rules as the big money campaigns of Election Industry, Inc.

Generate Free Press by Generating Talk Value

It's a firmly held adage in marketing communications that the best advertising is word of mouth. If you hear from a friend or someone like yourself that such-and-such is a good product, or so-and-so is an interesting candidate, you are more likely to believe it and try that product or pay attention to that candidate so you can then judge for yourself. And if what you hear turns out to be true, you will likely pass along the good word to friends of *yours*.

When people are talking about something, the press tends to take notice and do stories about that something. Why? Because it's what their readers want to read about, it's what their listeners want to hear about, and it's what their viewers want to see. It's what is interesting to people. By definition, it's *news*. Whenever a candidate "comes out of nowhere" or "really has momentum in this race," inevitably it is due to this kind of a phenomenon—creating positive talk value, or "buzz," which then leads to press stories, which leads to more buzz, which leads to more follow-up stories.

In this way, free press (or "earned media," as the public

relations professionals like to call it) can help to overcome the advantages your opponent may have in dollars and spending on paid media. What's more, recommendations from friends or stories from third parties such as the (supposedly) neutral press tend to have more credibility with the voters than paid media, which is largely dismissed as propaganda.

And there are even greater dividends to this approach. The same kind of imaginative and creative campaign communications that lead to positive word of mouth, greater media coverage, and greater momentum also lead to the dual benefits of more volunteers and more money. Create momentum and interest in your campaign, and more people want to jump on the bandwagon and be a part of it. Volunteers who have been toiling in anonymity suddenly are being recognized for being part of a high-profile campaign, and find they are getting hung up on less often when calling voters—people actually have an interest in what they have to say, in finding out more about the candidate and the campaign. This results in reenergized volunteers who can now work more effectively and will therefore work harder than ever.

And it leads to more money. Maybe everybody loves a winner, but the people who make large political contributions love winners most of all. Create interest and momentum, and more money inevitably flows into the campaign. Contributors who had been sitting on the sidelines now see a functional, credible campaign. Contributors who gave to your opponents now smell another potential winner and decide they'd best hedge their bets by giving to you, too. A multiplier effect kicks in: like your volunteers and field workers, your fundraisers suddenly find it easier to get phone calls returned, more people who want to attend events, more people who will host fundraisers.

As you can see, it's an amazingly cost-effective strategy.

Word-of-mouth is not only the best kind of advertising there is, it's also the cheapest.

But in order to do all this, first you must be interesting to people. And as innumerable political campaigns have proven, money can't buy that.

Achieve Critical Mass in Your Fundraising

All of this is not to say that you can accomplish something with nothing. I've never done a winning race where the campaign had no money whatsoever. Unless you can compile a critical mass of funds—enough money to have a functional and credible campaign—the best you can do is create interest for a brief period of time.

Candidates who never achieve critical mass are the candidates and the campaigns that "flame out"—who seemed to momentarily have an opportunity to win, but couldn't sustain public interest. In most elections, you need some money to afford at least some paid media—often this is what creates the original interest in the campaign and seeds word of mouth. You need some money to run a functional operation and establish credibility with the press. And you need resources to capitalize on the interest and momentum you generate—your field organization, your volunteers, your phoners, your canvassers have to get the vote out on Election Day, or whatever miracles you have performed without sufficient money will ultimately be for naught.

Invest in an Effective Field Organization

Most progressive candidates, and nearly all underfunded candidates, fall in love with the romantic notion of an all-volunteer, grassroots campaign. "We'll overcome their money with shoe leather and an army of committed volunteers," cry out these Don Quixotes of the political world, only to come to the ultimate realization that in today's world of mass communications, even the most committed army on the ground is worthless without support in the air.

But many, many rich candidates have heeded the siren call of Election Industry, Inc., spending huge amounts of money on dull, vapid commercials and poorly conceived media buys, only to come to realize that even the best air campaign is worthless without the ground troops to get the voters to the polls.

It's a truism that underfunded campaigns have more volunteers, and more committed volunteers than most heavy-spending, media-driven campaigns. But the greater truth is that one is not a substitute for the other—today, you need both. The most cost-effective campaigns are those that do their media well but cheaply, while investing a sufficient amount of financial resources in the field organization to make sure that come Election Day, all that persuading will not have been pointless.

★ ★ ★
Use the Internet Effectively

The Internet provides some powerful opportunities for underfunded candidates and campaigns. Especially combined with accurate targeting, a well-conceived internet communications strategy can compete quite effectively with a big-budget paid media campaign.

A strong web-based communications campaign contains many of the elements of strong word of mouth. Putting paid media messages and press releases on your website extends their reach. Making them downloadable or able to be forwarded and passed around over the internet extends their reach exponentially—a virtual grassroots tool.

Fundraising via your website is about the cheapest way I've seen to raise money. And a good web-based campaign can operate a "virtual" field organization, saving a lot of time and money on communications and activities that would otherwise have to be paid for or done by volunteers.

And assuming the recently enacted McCain-Feingold campaign reform legislation holds up in court, there are many new financial advantages and exclusions for internet-based communications versus paid mass media communications.

Advocate for Debates, and Take Advantage of the Opportunity They Present

Underfunded candidates can rarely afford to get out their own positive messages while also effectively contrasting themselves with their opponents. So the contrast has to come from something other than paid media.

Debates offer the best opportunity to do this cheaply. If the debate is broadcast, you are on the airwaves and you don't have to pay for the airtime.

Best of all, debates give the voters a chance to see you as you really are, without the strangling time limits of a sixty-second radio commercial or a thirty-second television spot. And the voters not only get to experience you in context with the other candidates, they can make direct comparisons—comparisons where you can draw clear distinctions and differences between yourself and your opponents.

Most underfunded candidates are challengers, and debates are essential for challengers. Debates do not allow incumbents to ignore their challengers and to rely instead on superior financial resources and name recognition to win an easy election. Debates are one of the few campaign instances where incumbents and challengers are on the same level playing field, if only for the duration of the debate.

There's no arguing the benefits of debates for underfunded candidates.

☆ ☆ ☆
Jujitsu Your Opponent

Jujitsu is the Japanese martial art where you use your opponent's superior size and weight against him. The same can be done with money in politics.

Underdog candidates need to claim the moral high ground in a campaign. We did this very successfully in Paul Wellstone's 1990 election, by insinuating that his opponent was trying to buy the election. It was so successful that every time one of the incumbent's many commercials appeared, voters saw it as another example—and positive proof—of the incumbent's strategy to swamp Wellstone financially and buy the election.

Many big-spending candidates—and especially incumbents utilizing fundraising firms straight out of Election Industry, Inc.—receive campaign contributions from individuals or organizations with a checkered past. Often you can scour their campaign finance reports and find contributors that will embarrass the campaign when they are made public. (Of course, you have to make sure your list of contributors is above reproach before implementing this strategy.)

Be Creative in Your Media Planning and Placement

A typical Election Industry, Inc. strategy for incumbents is to adopt an imperial strategy and ignore the opponent until late in the campaign, then unleash a late saturation TV buy that the underfunded challenger has no chance of matching.

It's a valid strategy, but it leaves the media stage empty for most of the election. In 1990, we took advantage of this to run Paul Wellstone's commercials in a media vacuum. We had little money to spend, but the effect of the money was magnified because Wellstone's were the only commercials being seen for the U.S. Senate race. (And they were the only political commercials of any stripe being noticed, because they weren't anything like the formulaic political commercials for candidates in other races airing at the same time.) If the incumbent had aired even a smattering of his own commercials in that time period, it might have negated ours, and certainly would have mitigated the rapid progress we were making by having the stage to ourselves.

Some candidates are what I call "short-fuse" candidates; others are "long-fuse." (This has nothing to do with their tempers, by the way.) Wellstone was a long-fuse candidate. Because he had little experience running for office and even less name recognition, he needed time to develop a persona with the voters. The fuse had to be lit a long way out from Election Day in order to get the kind of explosion we wanted at the right time. This also allowed the Wellstone campaign to develop their volunteers and field organization and gave them time to reach a critical mass of funding. Wellstone needed the

1990 race to be a marathon, not a sprint. He couldn't have won a sprint.

In contrast, Jesse Ventura was a short-fuse candidate. He was already a household name, with an established personality, familiar to millions from his days as a professional wrestler. He was extremely media savvy as well. While his campaign needed time to develop a viable strategy and some momentum, a candidate like Ventura can win when the race is reduced to a short track, even with very little money.

You can usually use the predictability of Election Industry, Inc. against it. As in the Wellstone race, we looked for empty stages where Ventura could dominate. Because we knew where his opponents were going to advertise, we were able to find and exploit holes in their strategy. We were also able to elbow our way onto the sold-out shows where *they* were advertising by exploiting another vulnerability in their media plans—the equal time and equal access provisions. Most campaigns work to place their TV buys from Election Day backwards, to make sure they get the most important time slots they want closest to Election Day. But one of the Achilles' heels in the carpet-bombing media strategies of Election Industry, Inc. is the equal access provision in election law. During Ventura's campaign, because the other two campaigns had been buying tons of TV time for weeks, we saw we would be in a position to invoke equal access to the programs they had been buying. That means if they had a spot placed on, say, *ER* in prime time the Thursday before the election, and they had been running a spot on *ER* for a number of weeks, we could demand that the station sell us a spot on *ER* at the same rate. Best of all, if the station didn't have any more spots available on *ER* that night, *they would have to remove one of the other campaigns' spots and give us that time slot.*

So by precisely timing our media strategy and ad buys, we

were effectively able to *double* our ads' impact: not only did we get a high-profile time slot at the lowest rate just days before the election, we managed to remove one of our competitor's ads at the same time.

That's the kind of creative media thinking that leads to big, *big* upsets.

Looking Forward and Moving Ahead

D espite having spent a little bit of time on the staff of a U.S. senator—and discovering that many, many people in government do work very, very hard—the ins and outs of legislative and policy maneuvering in Washington bore me. It is all heat and no light—a lot of evanescent sound and fury around incremental measures that rarely have a major effect on most peoples' lives.

This is not to say it is not important work. Of course it is. Like most Americans, I believe it could be done more cheaply and more efficiently, but this does not diminish its importance. Are people hurt by decisions made in the White House and on Capitol Hill? Every day. Do people and corporations and even entire industries get rich on the basis of decisions made in Washington? You bet they do. (That's why there's a K Street in Washington—for all the special interest lobbyists and lawyers officed there who believe the "K" stands for "$1,000.")

Creating large-scale reform in Washington is very difficult. It's a catastrophe of *kakistocracy*—government by the worst elements of the system. The entire area is beholden to the federal government, and when people have been around government for so long, the status quo starts to look pretty good. After all, they figure, if we could do better as a country, we certainly would have by now.

In her book *Washington,* the late Meg Greenfield, a longtime reporter and political columnist, observed that life in Washington most resembles life in high school. That's pretty accurate. Our politics have been reduced to popularity contests between preening, vacant candidates; and the Holy Grail that every party and pollster and consultant and candidate searches for in every election is some oversimplified slogan that can be attached to these candidates to make them more popular.

Though the two major political parties and the rest of Election Industry, Inc. will be the last to realize it, more and more Americans could care less about political parties and party ideology.

Our national *anomie* is the natural outcome of Election Industry, Inc.'s insatiable quest for money. Most people don't have the financial wherewithal to make big political contributions to political candidates and political parties. Consequently, both of our major political parties—and their candidates—have turned ever more increasingly to special interest groups, to professional fundraisers, to wealthy individuals, and to political action committees to subsidize their campaigns for public office.

Not only has this narrowed the traditional differences between the two parties, it has spawned a peculiar breed of candidate—in both parties—that is anything but a leader. Because these candidates and their parties are indentured to so many rich contributors and special interest groups, they go out of their way not to offend any of these people, who are their true constituencies. Meanwhile, candidates and party platforms are driven by poorly designed polls and insulated political consultants, whose only goals are to get candidates elected and keep their meal ticket of a political party in power. The true voice of the people never gets through, not to the party nor to the candidate.

That's not leadership; it's pandership.

People in this country are not stupid. Our citizens see that most elections are devoid of meaningful differences between the candidates, and that most candidates lack anything remotely resembling the quality we used to call "leadership." Citizens see the continuous quest for campaign cash, and they know that the candidate standing in front of them is looking well past them for the next funder, even as that candidate shakes your hand and pretends to listen. Our citizens know that most political speeches are mere ear candy, filled with poll-tested pandering designed to placate the masses, while being empty of anything meaningful or nutritional that could affect or enrich their daily lives.

America's citizens have also learned that despite the lip service and the platitudes, the true purpose of our two major parties is definitely *not* to involve as many voters as possible in the democratic process.

So why are we surprised that people in America have insulated their lives against politics? They no more look to Washington to solve their problems than they would pray to the man in the moon and expect results. People have turned inward, especially those of Generation X and Generation Y who can't believe what a mess the baby boomers have made of this country.

Younger Americans look to their families and friends and to their neighbors—people in their local communities—to solve problems in their little part of the world. What they want most from Washington is to be left alone. "Just don't make our lives any more difficult than you already have" is their attitude. By ignoring Washington, their most fervent hope is that they will be treated in kind.

Despite the dire proclamations of the occasional secretary of state each election period, I don't think the two major parties see declining voter participation as a big concern, and certainly Election Industry, Inc. doesn't. As more and more money gets spent on a shrinking pool of voters, their methods of persuasion can become more and more focused and effective.

If things continue on this course, at some point in the future we may have each party and each presidential candidate spending their entire billion-dollar campaign budgets trying to persuade one person in Wyoming—let's call him Bob—who was the slowest to catch on and is therefore the last and only person voting in America.

To save Bob from that horrible fate, here are a few things we can do right now to make our democracy more inclusive:

☆ ☆ ☆

Get the money out

I don't know anybody who has come up with the ideal solution yet, but if the highest and best goal of a participatory democracy is to have the greatest number of people actively involved in the way they are governed, it's obvious that the system we have right now isn't working. Our country was founded on the basis that all of us are equal: rich and poor, black and white, religious and nonreligious. Yet our courts have ruled that political spending is equivalent to political speech. How can this be? As a candidate, how am I equal to a competitor who can spend a hundred times what I can afford to spend? As a voter in a system of representative government, how does my vote count with my representative as much as the vote of someone who contributes thousands of dollars to that representative's campaign?

The playing field should be level. Set a reasonable upper limit for what can be spent on campaigns for particular offices. Will incumbent politicians and the rich still have a built-in advantage? Yes. Will some candidates still be able to spend one hundred times more than others? Yes. But without any reasonable upper limit, this ridiculous "how high is up?" notion that candidates can spend as much as they want to get elected is leading to a nation that is governed by the rich, not by the people.

During the 2000 election cycle $3,000,000,000 was spent on political campaigns. That's not a typo. That's *three billion* dollars And about $1 billion of that was spent on ads. It's a growth industry, too—as recently as the 1996 election cycle, "only" $500 million was spent on political ads.

No wonder political consultants and TV stations are smiling when the even-numbered years come around.

During the 2000 election cycle, the Republican Party spent $78.3 million on so-called "issue" ads, generally designed to provide support for their candidates. It was a very good fundraising cycle for the Democrats, too. The Democratic Party spent $78.2 million. (So apparently whoever says there's not a dime of difference between the two parties is wrong—it looks like there's about $100,000 worth of difference.)

Today, going rates in the marketplace of politics are $60 million and up for a Senate seat; $50 million or more to be mayor of New York; up to $4 million for a seat in Congress.

I live in Minnesota. In 2000, we had an independently wealthy candidate basically buy a U.S. Senate seat, in a race that cost him between $12 million and $14 million, nearly all of that money going for ads.

To me, that is mind-boggling. Minnesota had the third

most expensive U.S. Senate race in the country in 2000, trailing only Jon Corzine's bloated-but-narrow $60 million victory (against an opponent who spent only $5 million) in the expensive New Jersey media markets, and the megabucks Hillary Clinton campaign in New York.

I have been in the ad business in Minnesota for a very long time. I don't know a single commercial advertiser who would spend $14 million on advertising *in a year*—much less over a few months—in Minnesota alone. (And remember, federal candidates for office are guaranteed the lowest ad rates on any given station, so political dollars go a lot further than commercial dollars.)

I honestly don't know how anybody could efficiently spend $12 million in Minnesota, short of just giving the money to the two million or so voters who regularly show up at the polls. I'm an advertising expert and I couldn't spend that much money. And I don't mean out of conscience—I mean I *literally* wouldn't know how to do it.

By way of contrast, when we did all the media buying for Paul Wellstone's 1996 reelection—the state's previous Senate race—he spent no more than $6 million on advertising, and I was begging the campaign in the final three weeks not to send us any more money. They didn't need to spend any more, and I didn't know where to put it. (Wellstone won easily, by nearly 10 percentage points, or 200,000 votes.) In 1990, Wellstone spent far less than $1 million in media advertising to get elected.

If you don't think these costs have rocketed out of control, just review the math.

Enforce the laws

If we are not going to require that TV and radio stations give candidates free advertising time, we should at least make sure that the ad rates candidates pay are protected.

A lot of laws that apply to the rest of the country don't apply to Congress. But Congress, in its inestimable wisdom, did make a law back in 1971 that benefits people running for federal office. That is the lowest unit rate, or lowest unit cost, regulation for political ad time.

In its simplest terms, this regulation allows political candidates (but not necessarily political parties or other special interest groups) to purchase ad time at the lowest cost any commercial advertiser paid for that same time slot anytime during the previous year.

Obviously, this makes politicians' ad dollars go much farther, and allows them to fill the airwaves with even more of the crappy ads we've learned through the years to despise.

Stations have figured that out. And while they like the money, they also realized that a steady diet of political ads was a big reason why people switch stations. So, in violation of the law, they started to play all sorts of games with their ad sales policies. They restricted political ad time to specified time slots, "ghettoizing" political ads in, say, the last five minutes of the evening news.

Then they artificially created entirely new classes of times and rates which rarely apply to any advertising other than political commercials. Consequently, you might pay different rates for the same exact time slot on the same exact program depending upon whether you bought it on a *preemptible* basis, a more expensive rate if you buy it on a *preemptible with notice* basis, and a higher rate still if you bought the ad on a *nonpre-emptible* basis.

Stations unilaterally imposed these new classes of time, and the huge majority of political media consultants simply shrugged their shoulders. Why would they complain? They get compensated on the basis of a percentage of how much money their candidates spent on advertising. So the more the candidates needed to spend, the more the consultants made. Rather than fighting it or suggesting that candidates buy less ad time or move dollars into different media, political media consultants and their media buyers were directly complicit with the stations in ripping off their own candidates.

Consultants simply acquiesced to the higher rates and told candidates it would be that much more expensive to reach the threshold for the amount of TV advertising required to win. This meant candidates had to go out and raise even more money, which meant our democratic system was evermore at the mercy of rich campaign contributors and special interest groups.

Because we so often work for underfunded and under-dog candidates, my company has become expert in challeng-ing stations on the rules of equal time, equal access, and low-est unit cost charges. Many of our candidates have received substantial rebates in the tens or even hundreds of thousands of dollars because of our diligence.

In fact, during the 2000 election period, we worked closely with the Alliance for Better Campaigns to expose these station practices and to shine a light on those stations that were prof-iteering on political advertising. We provided the Alliance with our expertise and actual invoices to show the discrepan-cies in rates. The result was a scathing report, *Gouging Democ-racy: How the Television Industry Profiteered on Campaign 2000*, published in February of 2001 (the complete findings can be seen at www.bettercampaigns.org).

Of course, Congress was not too pleased when they found out what was going on. On March 21, 2001, barely a month after these practices were exposed, the Senate voted overwhelmingly (69–31) to require TV stations to offer discounted air time to candidates on a non-preemptible basis.

(If only we could get them to act so quickly on matters involving us . . .)

But the problem isn't just with the media. The Federal Election Commission (FEC) is also to blame.

I have watched the FEC's rulings over the past decade or so, and I have been amazed at what little deterrent effect its penalties have on political parties and candidates. Their slaps on the wrist amount to pats on the back.

Political parties and candidates regularly abuse the system to the tune of millions of dollars each election cycle, and generally end up with no more than a $10,000 fine. Two years after the fact.

Not one election result has ever been overturned because the winning political party or the winning candidate openly violated campaign financing laws.

Of course, who benefits from this system? Incumbents. And who makes the laws that the FEC is supposed to enforce? Incumbents. And who appoints the members of the FEC? You guessed it: incumbents and their political parties.

☆ ☆ ☆
Take back the airwaves

Making these reforms would have been a lot easier prior to our elected representatives giving away the store in the Telecommunications Act of 1996.

Broadcast frequencies for digital television (that long-awaited High Definition Television you've been hearing about for so long) were worth a lot of money when the government created them in the mid-1990s. If they were auctioned off instead of given away, conservative estimates put their value to broadcasters at anywhere between $20 and $50 billion.

Instead, our elected officials decided to hand them over free of charge. And in a remarkably bipartisan fashion. President Bill Clinton ignored his economic advisers and the FCC chairman at the time to go along with the scheme. Trent Lott, the Senate majority leader at the time, also thought it was a great idea. (Of course, he went to college with the man who was president of the National Association of Broadcasters at the time.)

How did the broadcasters get away with this? The usual tactics: money and intimidation. Politicians were cowed when the broadcasting lobby suggested that elected officials might not get much news time if they didn't hand over the frequencies, and politicians—especially incumbent politicians—depend on the media to carry their messages to constituents.

Of course, it didn't hurt that the broadcast industry contributed about $3 million to members of Congress in the 1996 election cycle, either.

The broadcasters lobby also ran commercials insinuating that if the frequencies went to auction, it would be the end of free broadcast TV.

Well, there's a rather serious flaw in that thinking. In case you didn't know this, the public controls the airwaves. We're the landlords. We license TV and radio stations and telecommunications businesses to use the airwaves *in the public interest.* They're the tenants.

We have had free over-the-airwaves broadcasts of radio and TV in this country since the technology was invented. Can you imagine how angry people would be if stations decided to try to charge for this? And since we happen to own the airwaves, if broadcasters ever decide to abandon free broadcasts, we will have a long, salivating line of people and corporations ready to take their places. Besides, exactly how many legislators do you think would allow this to take place if their constituents were 100 percent against it?

You might be surprised at the names of the heroes who advocated an auction and tried to stand in the way of the give-away. Former presidential candidate Bob Dole was one. And Senator John McCain—not so surprisingly—was the main advocate for the people.

Well, whatever Congress does, they should be able to undo. In the public interest, let's take back the airwaves for more debates and free airtime for candidates. That's certainly one way to get some of the big money out of the system and a good way to expand the number and types of candidates we can hear from.

Open up debates

Since Lincoln vs. Douglas back in the nineteenth century, debates have been a proud part of this country's political heritage and one of the best ways for voters to compare and to question candidates.

Radio and TV debates are today's version of soapbox debates in the town square. They are relatively inexpensive and at least partially unvarnished ways for voters to hear from and get to know candidates.

So why don't we make it mandatory that the major networks set aside time for nationally televised debates, and that local stations set aside time for candidates in statewide and congressional elections?

One reason is that, even though we own the airwaves and every TV and radio station is licensed to use those airwaves in the public interest, the stations don't like to lose ad revenue for the prime time slots they contribute for debates. The broadcasting lobby is one of the most powerful special interest groups in Washington. Their lobbyists and political action committees (PACs) are huge contributors to the two major political parties and to politicians already in office. Those incumbents don't pass laws requiring this because, as discussed earlier in this book, incumbents don't like debates. And incumbents write the laws and make the rules.

And please, spare me the dithering and hand wringing over who belongs in the debates and who doesn't. It's not that difficult. If people want to hear from a particular candidate, that candidate belongs in a debate.

People wanted to hear Ross Perot. They wanted to hear Jesse Ventura. People wanted to hear Pat Buchanan and Ralph Nader as well.

While we're at it, let's put the debates back into the hands of neutral third parties—let's not leave it up to the two major parties and their corporate sponsors to tell us who can be in the debates. By limiting access to debates, in a very real sense, they are deciding for us who our next president will be—or at least giving us only *their* choices.

☆ ☆ ☆
Count every vote!

We are the most technologically advanced country in the history of the world. Why are we still dealing with dangling chads and all sorts of other electoral tomfoolery? How hard can it be to find one system of voting and implement it across the country? So that whether you live in Walla Walla, Washington or West Palm Beach, Florida, on Election Day, you can be confident your vote and every other vote is going to be properly tallied and counted.

Find the most accurate system currently in use. See if there are any ways to make it even better. Set up a contest offering a million dollar prize if any inventor or company in America can come up with an even better system. Then implement the very best system we can find, uniformly, all across the country.

Is this going to cost money? Sure. And it should come from the federal government, not from the states, in order to make sure every polling site in the country can afford state-of-the art technology, regardless of how rich or poor its tax base.

This is money we should have been spending over the past century to continually improve and refine the accuracy of our elections. So no matter how expensive it is to do now, it's a one-time catch-up expense for decades of neglect. After all, in a democracy, what could be more important than the accuracy of elections?

Besides, if we don't do this, we may have to live through another election like the 2000 presidential race.

And you don't want to do *that* again, do you?

Adopt same-day voter registration

We've come a long way from Jim Crow laws and other attempts to deny certain people the right to vote. But we haven't come far enough.

Voter registration should be standardized across the country the same way voting technology should be standardized. If you are a citizen above the legal voting age, and you want to vote on Election Day, you should be allowed to vote on Election Day.

Those states that have same-day voter registration regularly have the highest voter turnout in elections. That's no accident. Especially in today's harried world, Election Day can sneak up on people. Who has the time to go register to vote weeks or months ahead of time?

The counterargument you hear from states without same-day voter registration is that it will lead to widespread election fraud.

That's simply not true. In fact, in most of the states with same-day voter registration, the occurrences of widespread voter fraud in elections have been either few or none—and certainly not as frequent as states *without* same-day voter registration.

It's simple. Either we want everyone who has a right to vote to be able to exercise that right, or we don't. If we do, we need to make it as easy as possible for citizens—every citizen—to vote on Election Day.

Help further democratize our elections by instituting instant runoff voting

If we really want to increase voter participation, and if we want to make every citizen feel that her or his voice is being heard, we should move to instant runoff voting—ranking every candidate on the ballot in the voter's order of preference.

The two major political parties will have a major problem with this, but the reason many people don't show up to vote is that they are purists who want to vote for the best person, not make some tortured choice between "lesser evil" candidates. It is precisely these types of voters who are most affected by "wasted-vote" arguments. If they don't like any of the choices, or if they believe their favored candidate cannot possibly win, they just stay home.

Today, when you cast your vote, it's all or nothing. The person you vote for gets all, and other candidates on the ballot get nothing.

But that leads to candidates winning who have no mandate, and who are seen as polar opposites and mortal enemies by the people who voted for their opponents. Democracy is about compromise and about doing the most good for the most people without penalizing those in the minority. So why not make it easier for the electorate to get behind and support the victor? The system we have now only heightens the partisan nature of our duopolistic political system and makes compromise and governing more difficult.

If we allowed voters to rank candidates, voters will still always choose their favorite candidate first, but they would also rank their second and third choices, and so on. Then no candidate could be termed a "wasted vote," no candidate would become a "spoiler," and everyone voting could feel better about having had full input into the final results. It would also serve as an incentive for more voters to learn more about all the candidates.

By the way, this is not a new idea in a democracy. It has been successfully used in places like Ireland, Australia, London, and other parts of the world for many years.

☆ ☆ ☆

Open up ballot access

Ranking candidates to make every vote count to its fullest doesn't help that much unless more candidates can get on the ballot.

Right now, there are tremendous obstacles to independent, alternative, and third-party candidates who want to run for office. The two major parties know that you can't get elected if you can't get on the ballot—not too many write-in campaigns succeed—and the people who control access to the ballot in most states are Republicans and Democrats. So they make it as difficult as possible for candidates who are not Republicans or Democrats.

Ballot access rules are arcane and different from state to state. It's another area where standardization is called for.

If we want to truly democratize our elections, we can't require candidates for public office to pay outrageous filing fees or collect unreasonable numbers of signatures. This is just Jim Crow under a different name.

Either we want to be a full-scale democracy, or we don't. If we want to involve more citizens in our government, and in our elections, we should start with these reforms.

In the immortal words of the late John "Bluto" Belushi of *Animal House* fame, who's with me?

Afterword

t was past midnight in late November 2002, and I was standing—all alone—in the Rotunda of the United States Capitol, looking up at the magnificent paintings and friezes encircling this majestic space. I'm not a religious person, but this was the closest thing I'd had to a religious experience in the past twenty-five years.

Certain windows on the Senate side of the Rotunda frame the lighted Capitol dome against the moonlit sky in ways that could not have been accidental. I don't know how many other Americans have ever had our Capitol all to themselves, but as I walked among the statues of former vice presidents, sat on the old, hard, worn wooden benches, and chatted with bored Senate staff and security who wanted nothing more than to go home, I was moved beyond belief.

U.S. Senator Paul Wellstone was dead. Less than four weeks earlier, my former candidate and friend had perished in a fiery plane crash in the woods of northern Minnesota, changing the entire tenor of the 2002 midterm elections. And Minnesota Governor Jesse Ventura was on his way out of office. Hounded by a hostile local press corps and by the two major political parties—who could agree on nothing except that they wanted him gone—Jesse had decided in June not to seek a second term.

For the previous hour and a half, I had been walking the hallways of the empty Capitol, waiting for my current boss, U.S. Senator Dean Barkley (I-Minn.), to complete his work in presiding over the waning moments of the 107th Congress. Except for a handful of security personnel, a smattering of Senate staffers, Democratic Majority Whip Harry Reid (D-Nev.), and a couple of Republicans left behind to argue with him, everybody else had departed town and wouldn't return until the end of the lame-duck session and the beginning of the 108th Congress.

I had agreed to do for the freshly minted Senator Barkley what I had never agreed to do for any of my candidates—work in a staff position. After Senator Wellstone's untimely and unexpected death just four days before Election Day, Governor Ventura had appointed Dean Barkley, director of planning for the state of Minnesota, to serve out the rest of the late senator's term.

Dean had called me on Election Day and asked me to meet with him that night. He had only forty-eight hours to put together a functioning Senate staff and head to Washington. By the end of our meeting, he had himself a director of communications.

I had never wanted to go to Washington or to work for four years or six years as part of an administration or on a legislator's staff. After all, I had a business to run, employees and clients who depended on me. Four to six years as a federal employee seemed more like a prison term than an opportunity.

But this was different. It would be, at most, six weeks, not six years. Republican Norm Coleman had been elected to succeed Wellstone, so there was no chance Barkley's term would be extended. It would give me an opportunity to experience public service and to view the workings of our government up close. It was an opening to see if there was any possibility to complete some of Paul's work or at least find a way to honor his memory. And it would be an opportunity to play an important role in major legislation, such as the upcoming Homeland Security bill, and potentially to be the deciding vote in a heretofore deadlocked 50/50 Senate. This kind of opportunity doesn't come along very often, I reasoned, and not only would it be interesting, it was also good leverage for the people of Minnesota.

In those six weeks in the Senate, here's what I saw and learned:

- A lot of our elected officials are every bit as phony as they seem.
- Nearly all our legislators are only as good as their staff members, who, in the true spirit of public service, often work incredibly hard for relatively little money.
- Political strategizing, partisanship, and special-interest lobbying hold far more sway in Washington than doing what's right for the people.
- The president, his cabinet, U.S. Senators, members of the House of Representatives, and occasional staff people are treated like royalty in Washington.
- We still have the greatest system of self-government the world has ever known.

In the past dozen years, I and the people I've worked with have been privileged to play a major role in some major political accomplishments. We've helped to expose the everyday legalized bribery that's considered business-as-usual political fundraising in Washington, and to effect some important reforms. We've shown how commonsense citizens and outside-the-box candidates can still win major public office, despite being grossly outspent and shunned by the two major parties. We've made political communications more interesting, more cost efficient, and much more effective.

We've helped to bring many people under the age of thirty-five into our system of participative democracy, and we've gotten people who'd never voted in their lives into a polling place for the first time. We've raised the profile of third-party candidates, demonstrated the importance of instant-runoff voting in being able to vote your conscience instead of your fears, and helped inject new ideas into the standard and tired partisan Democrat vs. Republican disagreements. Working for candidates like Paul Wellstone, Jesse Ventura, Ralph Nader, and others, we've helped to make progressive and populist politics, if not quite safe, at least possible again.

And we're not done yet.

In fact, if you think about it and connect the dots, it's only a matter of a few more election cycles before an Independent or third-party president is inevitable. Look at the successes of a Ross Perot, a Jesse Ventura, a John McCain, and yes, even an Arnold Schwarzenegger, and it's indisputable that either we are going to have far fewer people voting or we are going to have to provide voters with more and different candidates, political parties, viewpoints—in short, more choices.

There are many, many stories behind every political campaign—and every political commercial—far more than could fit within these pages. (In fact, the original manuscript for this book was half again as long as the book you're holding right now.) And plenty of stories remain to be told, such as:

- The many successes of the Ventura administration, successes made possible only by the election of a third-party governor not beholden to the Democratic or Republican parties or the special interests that control them
- The reasons why Ventura refused to run for a second term, and why that should concern anyone interested in changing our political system for the better
- The death of Paul Wellstone, and its national implications in affecting the 2002 midterm elections
- The coherent national strategy and successes of Republicans in those same midterm elections
- The disarray in the Democratic Party, and its inchoate, tone-deaf, brain-dead attempts to relate to voters since the 2000 presidential election
- The successes a truly Independent, non-beholden senator can have in Washington, D.C.
- The surprising account of how a political neophyte became mayor of Denver, Colorado, winning a nonpartisan election by the biggest margin in the history of the city
- The repercussions of the California recall election, and why Democrats still don't get it going into 2004

But those stories will have to wait for the next book.

If this book has held your interest this far, you owe it to yourself to see the commercials firsthand, either during one of my readings or speeches or at the websites www.North WoodsAdvertising.com or www.billhillsman.com. You'll find more stories, more case histories, and more of our commercials there as well.

Let's keep fighting to make America better.

Bill Hillsman
Minneapolis, MN
October 2003

☆ ☆ ☆ ☆ INDEX ☆ ☆ ☆ ☆

Page numbers in italics refer to the insert.

Index

Index

Index

Index

☆ ☆ **ABOUT THE AUTHOR** ☆ ☆

BILL HILLSMAN is CEO and Chief Creative Officer of North Woods Advertising, a marketing communications and political and public affairs consulting company based in Minneapolis. His work for Paul Wellstone's U.S. Senate campaign won the Grand EFFIE, awarded by the American Marketing Association for the most effective marketing and advertising campaign of 1990. His work for Jesse Ventura's gubernatorial campaign in 1998 and Ralph Nader's presidential campaign in 2000 received even more accolades. Bill has been named one of America's top one hundred marketing people, one of the fifty media people in America who most influence our world, and *Slate* magazine calls him "the world's greatest political adman."

Hillsman's commentary on marketing, advertising, and politics has appeared in the *New York Times*, NBC's *Today* show, National Public Radio, CNN, C-SPAN, *Slate* and *Salon* on-line magazines, *The Nation*, the British Broadcasting Company (BBC), and Japanese and German television. He has been profiled in *Newsweek, BusinessWeek,* and the *New York Times Magazine. Minnesota Law & Politics* listed him as one of Minnesota's 100 Most Influential People, as well as one of Minnesota's 100 Most Intelligent People, something he says people find truly amazing once they meet him.

9 781416 568339